Siskiyou County Schools
LIBRARY
Property of
SISKIYOU COUNTY SUPT. OF SCHOOLS OFFICE

CARIBBEAN SEA
BARBADOS
TRINIDAD AND TOBAGO
Port of Spain
CARACAS
Barranquilla
Cartagena
Maracaibo
Valencia
Ciudad Bolívar
Panamá
VENEZUELA
Georgetown
Paramaribo
Cayenne
GUYANA
SURINAME
FR. GUIANA
BOGOTÁ
Medellín
COLOMBIA
ISLA DEL COCO (Costa Rica)
ISLA DE MALPELO (Colombia)
Boa Vista do Rio Branco
GUIANA HIGHLANDS
ILHA DE MARAJÓ
Equator
ROCEDOS SÃO PEDRO E SÃO PAULO (Brazil)
Quito
ECUADOR
ARCHIPIÉLAGO DE COLÓN (GALÁPAGOS ISLANDS) (Ec.)
Guayaquil
Golfo de Guayaquil
Iquitos
Leticia
Manaus (Manáos)
Rio Negro
Rio Amazonas
Rio Solimões (Amazonas)
Belém (Pará)
São Luís (Maranhão)
Fortaleza (Ceará)
ARQUIPÉLAGO FERNANDO DE NORONHA (Brazil)
CABO DE SÃO ROQUE
Teresina
Natal
João Pessoa (Paraíba)
RECIFE (Pernambuco)
Maceió
Chiclayo
Trujillo
Pôrto Velho
Rio Branco
BRAZIL
PERU
LIMA
Callao
Cuzco
CHAPADA DE MATO GROSSO
Cuiabá
Brasília
Salvador (Bahia)
Arequipa
Mollendo
BOLIVIA
Sucre
Potosí
BRAZILIAN HIGHLANDS
Diamantina
Belo Horizonte
Vitória
Iquique
CHACO
PARAGUAY
Asunción
SÃO PAULO
Santos
RIO DE JANEIRO
CABO FRIO
Antofagasta
Tropic of Capricorn
Salta
Tucumán
Corrientes
Florianópolis
ISLA DE SAN FÉLIX (Chile)
ISLA DE SAN AMBROSIO
Copiapó
Coquimbo
Córdoba
Santa Fe
Salto
Pôrto Alegre
URUGUAY
Rio Grande
Valparaíso
SANTIAGO
Rosario
BUENOS AIRES
MONTEVIDEO
La Plata
Río de la Plata
ISLAS DE JUAN FERNÁNDEZ (Chile)
PAMPAS
Concepción
ARGENTINA
ANDES
CHILE
Bahía Blanca
Valdivia
Viedma
Golfo San Matías
Puerto Montt
ISLA DE CHILOÉ
Comodoro Rivadavia
Golfo San Jorge
ARCHIPIÉLAGO DE LOS CHONOS
FALKLAND IS. (ISLAS MALVINAS) (Br.)
Stanley
WELLINGTON
HANOVER
Río Gallegos
Estrecho de Magallanes
Punta Arenas
DESOLACIÓN
TIERRA DEL FUEGO
Mt. Sarmiento 8100
ISLA DE LOS ESTADOS
CABO DE HORNOS (CAPE HORN)
SOUTH GEORGIA (Falkland Is.)
SOUTH SANDWICH ISLANDS (Falkland Is.)
Drake Passage
SOUTH SHETLAND ISLANDS (B.A.T.)
SOUTH ORKNEY IS. (B.A.T.)
JOINVILLE
JAMES ROSS
Antarctic Circle
PACIFIC OCEAN
ATLANTIC OCEAN
0 200 400 600 800 1000 Miles
0 400 800 1200 1600 Kilometers
Scale 1:40 000 000; one inch to 630 miles.
Lambert's Azimuthal Equal Area Projection
Elevations and depressions are given in feet
Relief
Meters
Feet
3050 10 000
1525 5000
610 2000
305 1000
0 Sea Level 0
152.5 500
1525 5000
3050 10 000
6100 20 000
Longitude West of Greenwich
120° 110° 100° 90° 80° 70° 60° 50° 40° 30° 20° 10°
Copyright by Rand McNally & Co. R.L. 85-S-104

© Copyright by Rand McNally & Co. R.L. 85-S-104
PACIFIC OCEAN
ARCHIPIÉLAGO DE COLÓN
GALAPAGOS ISLANDS
ISLA DARWIN
ISLA WOLF
ISLA PINTA
ISLA MARCHENA
ISLA GENOVESA
ISLA ISABELA
Volcán Wolf
1646
Volcán Darwin
1280
FERNANDINA
Volcán La Cumbre
1463
ISLA SAN SALVADOR
ISLA BALTRA
ISLA PINZÓN
ISLA SANTA CRUZ
Bahía Isabel
Volcán Santo Tomás 1490
Cerro Azul 1689
Villamil
ISLA SANTA FE
ISLA SAN CRISTÓBAL
Puerto Baquerizo Moreno
El Progreso
ISLA SANTA MARÍA
ISLA ESPAÑOLA
GALÁPAGOS
(Ec.)
Equator
82°
80°
90°
6°
4°
PACIFIC
OCEAN
ISLA JICARÓN
CÉBACO
PUNTA MARIATO
PUNTA MALA
Jaqué
PUNTA MARZO
Golfo de Cupica
Golfo de Tribugá
Nuquí
CABO CORRIENTES
Bajo Baudó
Pichimá
PUNTA MAGDALENA
Buenaventura
ISLA GORGONA
Guapí
Mosquera
Ensenada de Tumaco
Tumaco
CABO MANGLARES
Bahía de Ancón de Sardinas
Valdez
Esmeraldas
PUNTA GALERA
Muisne
Daule
Santo Domingo de los Colorados
CABO PASADO
Bahía de Caráquez
Chone
Manta
CABO SAN LORENZO
Montecristi
Portoviejo
ISLA DE LA PLATA
Jipijapa
Quevedo
PUNTA SANTA ELENA
Salinas
Guayaquil
Milagro
Golfo de Guayaquil
ISLA PUNÁ
Puerto Bolívar
Machala
Tumbes
Zorritos
Máncora
PUNTA PEÑA NEGRA
Lobitos
Talara
PUNTA PARIÑAS
Sullana
Quito
Ibarra
Ambato
Riobamba
Babahoyo
Cuenca
Loja
Puyo
Tena
Baeza
MANABÍ
GUAYAS
ESMERALDAS
PICHINCHA
COTOPAXI
BOLÍVAR
LOS RÍOS
CAÑAR
AZUAY
EL ORO
LOJA
ZAMORA-CHINCHIPE
MORONA-SANTIAGO
PASTAZA
NAPO
TUMBES
PIURA
AMAZONAS
LORETO
CAQUETÁ
PUTUMAYO
NARIÑO
CAUCA
VALLE
CHOCÓ
ANTIOQUIA
CUNDINAMARCA
BOYACÁ
HUILA
TOLIMA
CALDAS
RISARALDA
SANTANDER
COLOMBIA
ECUADOR
PERU
Pasto
Ipiales
Popayán
Cali
Palmira
Tuluá
Buga
Armenia
Pereira
Manizales
Medellín
Bello
Itagüí
Envigado
Quibdó
Ibagué
Girardot
Neiva
Florencia
BOGOTÁ
Villavicencio
Tunja
Duitama
Chiquinquirá
Bucaramanga
Barrancabermeja
Puerto Berrío
La Dorada
SERRANÍA DE BAUDÓ
Puerto Asís
Puerto Leguizamo
Nuevo Rocafuerte
Tres Esquinas
Santa Rita
Cerro Cumare 720
Iquitos
Requena
Nauta
Omaguas
Intuto
Andoas
Barranca
Concordia
Borja
Santa Clotilde
Tarqui
Putumayo
Napo
Marañón
Ucayali

Enchantment of the World

ECUADOR

By Emilie U. Lepthien

Consultant for Ecuador: Murdo J. MacLeod, Ph.D., Professor of Latin American History, Department of History, University of Arizona, Tucson, Arizona

Consultant for Reading: Robert L. Hillerich, Ph.D., Bowling Green State University, Bowling Green, Ohio

Siskiyou County Schools
LIBRARY
Property of
SISKIYOU COUNTY SUPT. OF SCHOOLS OFFICE

CHILDRENS PRESS®
CHICAGO

Religious rituals, such as the wedding procession above, are important to the Ecuadorian Indians.

Library of Congress Cataloging-in-Publication Data

Lepthien, Emilie U. (Emilie Utteg)
Ecuador.

(Enchantment of the world)
Includes index.
Summary: An introduction to the geography, history, culture, industries, resources, and people of one of the smallest countries in South America.
1. Ecuador—Juvenile literature. [1. Ecuador]
I. Title. II. Series.
F3708.5.L47 1986 986.6 85-26967
ISBN 0-516-02760-3 AACR2

Copyright ©1986 by Regensteiner Publishing Enterprises, Inc.
All rights reserved. Published simultaneously in Canada.
Printed in the United States of America.
3 4 5 6 7 8 9 10 R 95 94 93 92 91 90 89

Photo Acknowledgments
Nawrocki Stock Photo: © Ulrike Welsch: Pages 4, 6; © Helmer: Cover, Pages 22 (left), 81; © Stuart Cohen: Page 89 (right); © D.J. Variakojis: Page 113 (top)
Victor Englebert: Pages 5 (right), 10 (right), 14, 18 (right), 23 (left), 25 (right), 40 (top), 45 (right), 56 (bottom left), 58 (left), 59 (left), 60 (left), 62, 63 (2 photos), 65 (2 photos), 68 (bottom), 70 (left), 74, 78, 84 (3 photos), 86 (2 photos), 94, 103 (2 photos), 105, 108, 113 (bottom left & right), 114 (left)
Tom Stack & Associates: © Gary Milburn: Page 5 (left)

For my beloved aunt, Alwiene O. Lehmann, a superior teacher

Chip & Rosa Peterson: Pages 8, 18 (left), 34, 38 (top), 40 (bottom), 72 (2 photos), 80 (right), 89 (left), 114 (right), 115 (2 photos); © Jim & Roxanne Sullivan: Page 12
Valan Photos: Pam Hickman: Pages 10 (left), 26 (right), 67; © Michel Bourque: Pages 13, 24, 38 (bottom left), 80 (left), 97 (2 photos), 101 (right); © Jean-Marie Jro: Pages 26 (left), 53, 58 (right), 59 (right), 83; © Herman H. Giethoorn: Page 28 (right); © R.D. Stevens: Pages 71, 101 (left)
Root Resources: © Evelyn Davidson: Page 11; © Art E. Langner: Page 25 (left); © Benjamin Goldstein: Page 27 (right); © Willis H. Helfrich: Page 38 (bottom right); © Jane P. Downton: Page 61 (left); © Irene E. Hubbell: Page 61 (right); © S. Domingo: Page 70 (right)
Gartman Agency: © Mel Zaboudek: Pages 15, 22 (right), 23 (right)
Emilie U. Lepthien: Pages 16, 56 (bottom right), 75, 90
Photri: Pages 27 (left), 45 (left)
Lynn M. Stone © 1985; Page 28 (left)
Hillstrom Stock Photo: © Steve Carr: Pages 30 (top), 92 (right); © Connie McCollum: Pages 56 (top), 60 (right), 68 (top)
Virginia Grimes: Pages 30 (bottom), 32, 92 (left)
Historical Pictures Service, Inc., Chicago: Pages 35, 36
Wide World Photo, Inc.: Page 50
Larry Reynolds Photography: Pages 91, 107
Len W. Meents: Maps on pages 9, 12, 15
Courtesy Flag Research Center, Winchester, Massachusetts 01890: Flag on back cover
Cover: Cuenca fruit and vegetable market

TABLE OF CONTENTS

The Sierra, or highlands, covers about one fourth of Ecuador.

Chapter 1

A COUNTRY OF CONTRASTS

The Republic of Ecuador (*República del Ecuador*) is crossed by the imaginary line around the earth that is equidistant from the North and South Poles. From that line's name—equator—the country derived its name.

Ecuador is one of the smallest countries in South America. Its size (109,484 square miles—283,561 square kilometers) is approximately that of the state of Colorado or the country of New Zealand. Colombia forms its northern border. Peru lies to the south and east. To the west swells the great Pacific Ocean.

Ecuador's towering dormant and active volcanoes, in parallel ranges of the Andes Mountains, contrast with the steamy jungles on the east and with the coastal area along the Pacific. Ecuador's fascinating *Archipiélago de Colón*—the Galápagos Islands—lies six hundred miles (one thousand kilometers) off the Pacific coast.

Ecuador's people, too, are diverse. Among them are Indians who lived in the country long before they were conquered by the Inca from Peru.

Chimborazo Volcano is the tallest mountain in Ecuador.

Spaniards heard of the great wealth of the Inca. Spanish conquistadores sailed along the west coast of South America, conquered the Inca, and ruled the land for almost three hundred years.

Finally the people of Ecuador attained their independence from Spain.

Indian tribes still farm in the Sierra and a few farm the Costa. The people of the Costa are peasants of many races. Small tribes still hunt and fish in the Oriente. The snowcapped peaks stand as mighty reminders of volcanic activity along the western coast of South America.

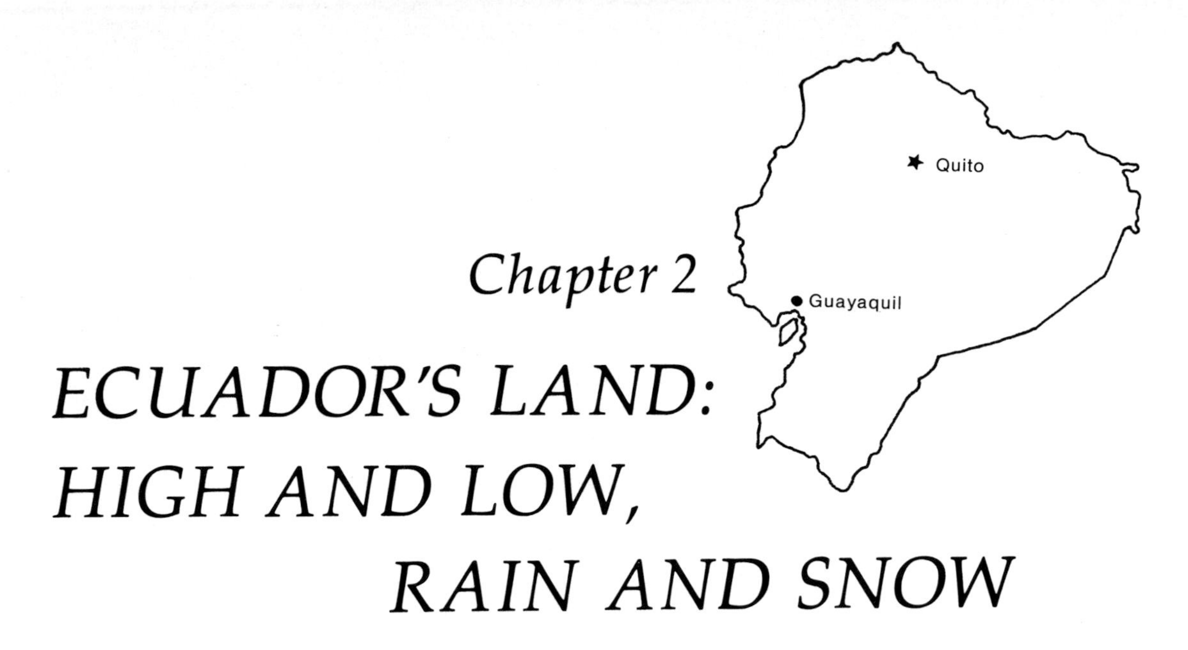

Chapter 2

ECUADOR'S LAND: HIGH AND LOW, RAIN AND SNOW

In Ecuador, the country on the equator, the sun is almost directly overhead throughout the year, especially at Quito, the capital.

The country should be very hot, and part of it is—the tropical rain forest near the northern coast. There is also steamy jungle east of the mountains. Guayaquil, the major seaport, is hot and humid.

But in the Andes, the spiny double backbone of the country, some peaks are snowcapped all year. In Quito the climate is springlike throughout the year.

THE HIGHLANDS: THE SIERRA

The mighty Andes, a backbone on the western side of South America, run from north to south through Ecuador. Two separate ranges have created a barrier for transportation and communication for centuries.

Fertile farming areas near Otavalo (left) and Riobamba (right)

The highlands region of Ecuador is called the Sierra. A plateau is cradled between the ranges. The average altitude of the plateau is 8,000 feet (2,650 meters). The Sierra is crossed by a hill system. The dozen or so fertile valleys between the two ranges of the Andes and these hills are called *hoyos.* In the fertile land of the *hoyos,* the Indians carefully till the soil and grow crops of potatoes, corn, and barley. Their fields have been farmed for centuries.

Many Indian groups live in the Sierra. Often they work for landowners who live in a city some distance away.

The Andes are of volcanic origin. On the west is the Cordillera Occidental. The eastern range with its mighty peaks is the Cordillera Central. The great trench or plateau between the two ranges, called the Avenue of the Volcanoes, is 50 to 80 miles (80 to 129 kilometers) wide. It covers about three eighths of the Sierra. Occasionally there are severe earthquakes in the area.

Cotopaxi, the world's highest active volcano

Twenty-two mighty peaks, from 14,000 feet (4,267 meters) to over 20,000 feet (6,096 meters) in altitude, thrust upward. There are lesser peaks as well. Of the thirty peaks of volcanic origin, six are still active. Sangay, over 19,000 feet (5,791 meters) high, is one of the world's most active volcanoes. Fumes and ash continually rise from its cone. Cotopaxi is the world's highest active volcano. From Riobamba, south of Quito, a glow in the sky can often be seen at night, a reminder that Cotopaxi is still alive.

Both a road and railroad run between Quito and Guayaquil on the coast. They traverse the Avenue of the Volcanoes. The route is spectacular. Unfortunately, part of the railroad bed was destroyed by heavy rains in 1982-83. Farms can be seen along the mountainsides even at altitudes of 12,000 feet (3,658 meters) above sea level. The Sierra occupies about one fourth of Ecuador's area.

Waterfalls in Baños, a health resort

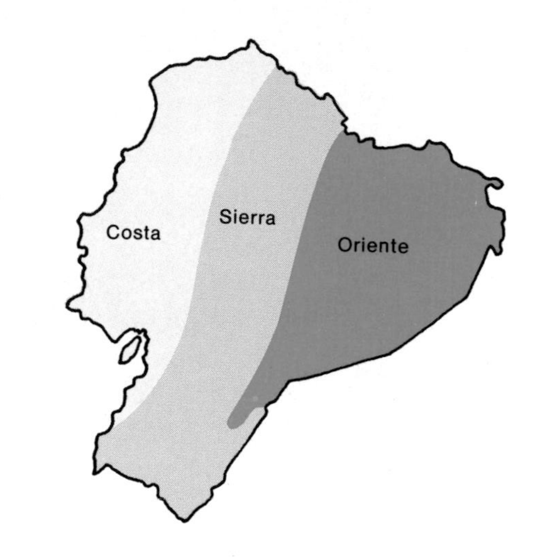

More than 45 percent of Ecuador's total population lives in the Sierra. Of Ecuador's almost nine million inhabitants, almost one million live in Quito, the capital.

If the present birthrate continues at 3.3 percent annually, the population will double in twenty-three years. Ecuador participated in the August, 1984 conference on population growth and its problems in Mexico City.

THE ORIENTE

Dropping down to the east from the Andes is the Oriente. This steaming jungle extends from the mountain foothills to the Upper Amazon basin. Dozens of mountain streams formed by melting snows and rains unite high in the Andes. Tumbling down thousands of feet, they become the tributaries of the mighty Amazon River.

The Río Arajuno flows through the jungle in the Oriente.

Although the Oriente makes up almost one half of the land area, only 3 percent of the population lives there. Many of the Indians retain their ancient customs. They are primarily hunters and fishermen. Some are hostile to intruders. Where jungle is cleared to provide small farms, the soil is so thin that it soon wears out. In a few years the farmers must move to new plots.

Petroleum has been found in the northern Oriente near Colombia. Producing wells have been drilled. The oil is pumped over the Andes and down to the west coast.

THE COSTA

The Costa is the coastal region along the Pacific Ocean. It is widest in the central section from Cape Pasado to Santa Elena

Guayaquil lies on the west bank of the Guayas River.

peninsula. At both the northern and southern end of the Costa, near the borders with neighboring Colombia and Peru, the area is narrow. The Costa ranges from 7 miles (11 kilometers) to 125 miles (201 kilometers) in width.

The Costa is the most prosperous of the mainland's three regions. It covers about one fourth of the country's total area. The most productive region is around Guayaquil, the largest city and principal seaport.

Most of Ecuador's tropical export crops are raised in this belt. However, in 1982 and 1983 heavy rains wiped out many of the crops. The economy was severely damaged.

A tropical rain forest is found in the northern Costa. But in the south near Peru almost no rain falls.

Over 50 percent of the population lives in the Costa. Guayaquil's population is well over one million. Other important coastal cities include San Lorenzo near the Colombian border, Esmeraldas, Salinas, Manta, and Machala.

Esmeraldas was named for the river in which emeralds were found. It is the fifth largest city and second largest port.

Bartolomé Island in the Galápagos

ARCHIPIÉLAGO DE COLÓN

Ecuador's fourth region is the famed *Archipiélago de Colón,* better known worldwide as the Galápagos Islands. That name comes from the Spanish word for the giant tortoises found on the islands—*galápagos.*

The equator runs through the archipelago, which lies 600 miles (970 kilometers) off the Pacific coast of Ecuador. The islands are inhabited by some of the most fascinating bird and marine life found anywhere in the world.

Formed from volcanoes, there are six major islands, twelve smaller islands, and more than forty islets. Only twelve thousand visitors are permitted each year. To view the fascinating wildlife, they must be accompanied by a naturalist-guide.

The ecology is so fragile that visitors must stay on paths, many of which have been laid out by the World Wildlife Fund. The Charles Darwin Research Station was built on Santa Cruz Island with the help of UNESCO (United Nations Educational, Scientific, and Cultural Organization). There the giant tortoises, which

Giant tortoises are protected at the Charles Darwin Research Station on Santa Cruz Island.

might otherwise have become extinct, are bred and raised in captivity. When they are about ten years old and able to defend themselves, they are released on the island from which their forebears came. Each island's tortoises are distinct.

The islands have a population of about six thousand humans. Most live in two small towns. In some cases, earlier settlers let cattle, goats, dogs, and cats run loose. They have become wild and often destroy precious wildlife.

For many years scientists debated about the origin of the islands. Had they once been connected to the mainland? Now it is agreed that they are the tops of volcanoes that rose out of the ocean and were never a part of the continent.

THE RIVERS

Ecuador's rivers rise in the Sierra. Most flow east toward the Oriente and become tributaries of the Amazon. Some are navigable for short distances in small craft.

Several rivers flow northwest or southwest. Río San Juan rises in western Colombia. It forms part of the boundary between the two countries.

The Santiago and Esmeraldas rivers in the northern part of the country are navigable for some distance inland. They have been panned for gold for many centuries.

Like the rest of the Pacific coast of South America, there are few natural harbors. Ports have been built, however, at several of the towns and cities. Few are of much importance for international shipping, except for Guayaquil and Esmeraldas.

Esmeraldas has a new commercial port. Exports include bananas and timber. Balao, ten miles (sixteen kilometers) south, handles petroleum. This port is growing in importance as oil is piped from the Oriente to an ocean terminal and a refinery.

Although other rivers enter the Pacific Ocean along the west coast, none is as important as the Guayas. It forms the largest river system on South America's Pacific coast.

High in the Andes the Guayas's headstreams begin their flow southwest. Its tributaries are extensive. The Chimbo alone is 125 miles (201 kilometers) long. The Daule begins west of Quito. It flows south through fertile farmlands before it joins the Guayas 175 miles (282 kilometers) from its beginning in the Andes. Part of the Daule is navigable.

The Guayas enters the Gulf of Guayaquil at a delta navigable by oceangoing vessels forty miles (sixty-four kilometers) upstream. Ecuador's largest city, Guayaquil, is thirty-three miles (fifty-six kilometers) upriver from the gulf. Its ocean port, ten miles (sixteen kilometers) from the city, was begun in 1959 and inaugurated in 1963.

Guayaquil handles more than 60 percent of Ecuador's foreign

Both Río Pastaza (left) and Río Napo (right) eventually join the Amazon River system.

trade. Almost half of the bananas, 40 percent of the coffee, all of the sugar, and almost all of the rice, cacao, shrimp, and balsa are shipped from Guayaquil's busy port. There are other exports as well. Guayaquil's port operates twenty-four hours a day throughout the entire year.

The rivers that flow eastward wend their way down to the Amazon. The Napo rises near Cotopaxi Volcano in northeastern Ecuador. Five hundred fifty miles (885 kilometers) later it enters the Amazon near Iquitos, Peru.

One of the Napo's tributaries is the Curaray. It, too, is over 500 miles (804 kilometers) long, flowing through some of the finest forests in South America. Like the Napo, it is navigable part of the way.

SEASONS

Ecuador is said to have two seasons: the dry season from June to December, and the rainy season from January through May.

The hottest months along the coast are during the rainy season, especially from February through April. In Guayaquil the two coolest months are August and September.

In the Sierra, the driest months are from June to September. In December they have what they call *veranillo*, or Indian summer. With an altitude of 9,000 feet (2,743 meters), Quito has a very pleasant climate year round. Quitonians call it "eternal spring."

CLIMATIC ZONES

Ecuador can be divided roughly into five climatic zones. They result from differences in altitude and location.

The tropical zone stretches from sea level to 3,000 feet (914 meters). In the northern and central Costa, temperatures and humidity are high throughout the year. Rainfall is generally heavy and there may be little wind.

The subtropical zone stretches from 3,000 feet (914 meters) to 6,500 feet (1,981 meters). Temperatures may be 10 degrees Fahrenheit (5 degrees Celsius) cooler than in the tropical zone. The Oriente is included in the subtropical zone, although a great portion of the region has an average altitude of only 800 feet (244 meters). The large forest area regulates the temperature.

The temperate zone is roughly 10 degrees Fahrenheit (5 degrees Celsius) cooler than the subtropical. It rises from 6,500 feet (1,981 meters) to 10,000 feet (3,048 meters). The temperature averages range from 63 degrees Fahrenheit (17.2 degrees Celsius) to 52 degrees Fahrenheit (11.1 degrees Celsius), depending upon the altitude. At the higher altitudes, the average temperature is lower.

The cold zone has average temperatures from 52 degrees Fahrenheit (11.1 degrees Celsius) down to 35 degrees (1.7 degrees Celsius) as the altitude rises from 10,000 feet (3,048 meters) to 15,000 feet (4,572 meters). These are the Sierras of the Andes.

High on the giant peaks, above 15,000 feet (4,572 meters), lies the frigid zone. Here the temperatures are so low that there is permanent snow and glaciers.

Ecuadorians boast that theirs is the only country in the world with both 0 degrees Celsius (32 degrees Fahrenheit) and 0 degrees latitude.

Of course, the zones are not lines that show marked changes. There are transition zones between them.

The Costa is a good example of differences in climate despite similar altitude. The differences are caused by rainfall, humidity, and temperature. At the northern end in Esmeraldas, there is an abundant rainfall, almost 100 inches (254 centimeters) annually. A tropical rain forest exists along the coast.

But near Santa Elena in the south Costa, rainfall is only 10 inches (25.4 centimeters) annually. This is a semiarid zone.

EL NIÑO

Approximately every six or seven years an unusual rainfall occurs along the coast. It is caused by El Niño. Since it usually begins around Christmas, it has been named for the Christ Child.

El Niño, a shift in ocean currents, is caused by changes in atmospheric pressure. Warm waters pour in toward South America. Usually winds blowing from the north combine with the rotation of the earth to send warmer Pacific coastal waters westward. But during El Niño the warmer waters are closer to shore. These warm seas bring heavy rains.

Generally El Niño lasts for only a few months. However, the worst "visitation" of El Niño occurred in 1982 and lasted through much of 1983. It influenced weather in many parts of the world. A severe previous El Niño was recorded in 1972-73. The impact on fishing and farming was great. But it did not compare with the destruction in 1982-83.

In Salinas, for example, January and February rainfall usually amounts to less than 2 inches (5 centimeters). In 1983 during those two months it was over 23 inches (58.9 centimeters). One of the bridges on the road between Guayaquil and Salinas was washed out, cutting off Salinas from the rest of the country for some time.

Guayaquil recorded its heaviest rainfall in history in March, 1983. El Niño was the culprit. It caused floods and landslides around the city. The destruction reached far above the Costa.

The average temperature of air and coastal waters, the tides, sea level, wave heights, and relative humidity all were much higher than normal.

Floods and landslides did terrible damage. Fourteen bridges were knocked down. Crops of cacao, bananas, rice, and pineapples and thousands of cattle were destroyed.

Hundreds of people died. Thousands of houses in Guayaquil and along the coast were destroyed. Then mosquitoes and other insects that breed in stagnant and polluted water carried disease to the devastated areas. Typhus, typhoid fever, and salmonella were prevalent.

The flooding finally stopped in July, 1983. But it would be a

Poincianas tree (left) and bromeliad blossoms (right)

long time before Ecuador would recover from the worst El Niño in its history.

FLORA

A tropical rain forest grows in the northern part of the Costa. Balsa and mahogany trees are found there as well as in the Amazon basin.

The cinchona tree, source of quinine used in treating malaria, grows in the tropical rain forest. This tree is so important to the health and economy of the country that it has been named the national tree. Palms are also abundant.

Beautiful flowering trees—acacias, royal poincianas, and magnolias—as well as orchids and bromeliads add color to the virgin forest.

Mangrove swamp (left), found near the coast, and angels trumpet (right), which grows on Santa Cruz Island

Vanilla, cinnamon, chicle, cedar, cypress, bamboo, and wild cherry are other native plants. Along the northern coastline and the Gulf of Guayaquil mangrove swamps are found in abundance.

Jungle plants supplied food and other necessities to the Indians for centuries before the conquering Spanish learned of their value. Today they still contribute to Ecuador's economy.

In the Sierra, pine, willow, and cypress are found. Eucalyptus trees have been introduced into the country. They were not native to Ecuador.

At the southern end of the Costa near Peru, scrublike vegetation dots the landscape. Cacti, mimosa, and chaparrel grow in this semiarid region. Grassy savannas and scrub forests cover much of the area.

In the mountain regions alpine plants flourish. Daisies, lupines, and herbs are abundant. Many of the plants are used as medicines.

Tree ferns along the Río Arajuno in the Oriente

High up on the mountainsides, above the timberline, only grayish or rust-colored lichens cover the rocks.

There are about two thousand different kinds of trees native to Ecuador. The number of plants is countless. Many never have been classified by botanists.

Because of scanty rainfall on the Galápagos Islands (*Archipiélago de Colón*), few trees can be found above 1,000 feet (305 meters). Half of the species of desert plants growing on the islands are found nowhere else on earth.

FAUNA

The forests, especially the rain forests, are home to many native animals. Most of the wildlife is found in the Oriente. But the northern Costa with its tropical rain forest also has a great variety of native animals.

Titis (left) and sloths (right) live in the forest and jungle regions.

In the rain forests, fewer people have intruded to destroy the natural habitat of the animals. Fewer animals have been hunted. The climate has also helped wildlife to survive.

Monkeys of all sizes, from the tiny titi to the large howler monkey, spend their lives in the forest.

In the jungle regions tapirs, anteaters, sloths, armadillos, and lizards are found. Dangerous snakes like the poisonous bushmaster and the fer-de-lance are encountered. Anacondas, often over twenty feet (six meters) in length, attack without reason. They strangle their victims. Anacondas spend much of their time in the rivers.

There are many smaller animals native to the country. Porcupine, opossum, rabbit, and squirrel are common. Jaguar, puma, and the small tigrillo can be seen generally in the highlands. The llama, first used by the Indians for wool and meat, lives in the Andes around Riobamba. The Inca used the llama as a beast of burden.

A mother llama with her kid (left) and a land iguana (right) in the Galápagos

Carnivorous animals include the fox, coatimundi, giant otter, raccoon, skunk, and weasel.

On the Galápagos Islands giant tortoises (*galápagos* in Spanish), land and marine iguanas, huge sea turtles, sea lions, and fur seals can be seen.

Many of Ecuador's animals are on the endangered species list. In 1970 a ban was placed on capturing any of these endangered species. Rules limit taking other species considered beneficial to man; a license is required to capture them.

Ecuador has one of the world's largest regulatory systems to protect wildlife.

BIRDS

About 1,500 species of birds have been classified. Some are seasonal. When it is winter in the Northern Hemisphere the

Blue footed boobies (left) and frigate birds nest on the Galápagos Islands.

scarlet tanager, various waterfowl, and the barn swallow, for example, spend a southern summer in Ecuador.

Ecuador's native bird life is very rich. Giant condors with wingspreads of 12 feet (3.6 meters), eagles, and hawks can be observed. In the tropical regions, parrots, macaws, toucans, herons, flamingos, and jacamars thrive. Ecuador is also home to many species of hummingbirds.

Some unique studies of bird life can be made on the Galápagos Islands. Each island has its own species of finch, particularly adapted to life on its own island. These differences were first noted by naturalist Charles Darwin. Blue footed and masked boobies and frigate birds nest on these islands.

One of the most interesting birds is the Galápagos penguin. The cold Humboldt Current sweeping up from the Antarctic makes

A flamingo (left), found in the tropical regions, and Galápagos penguins (right)

the waters habitable for this small species. No other species of penguins live this far north on the equator. The Galápagos penguins are seriously threatened when the waters are warmed even a few degrees by El Niño.

The flightless cormorant is another species unique to these islands.

FISH

Fish is essential in the diet of the Indians of the Oriente. In the freshwater rivers of that region, catfish and arapaima are caught. Rainbow trout have been introduced into these rivers.

The coastal waters, except during the devastating periods of El Niño, abound in fish. From January through April the migratory skipjack tuna are caught. Mackerel, snapper, haddock, sardines, thread herring, swordfish, and squid are common. Together with sea bass, these fish are important in Ecuador's fishing industry.

NATURAL RESOURCES

Recently developed oil fields in the Oriente are perhaps Ecuador's most important natural resource. But there are others that have played an important role in the country's history.

Ecuador's location on the western flank of the Andes gave promise of great mineral wealth. But the Spanish conquistadores and more recent prospectors have been disappointed.

The conquistadores sought gold. At first they found much in the southern section of the country. They named the province El Oro after the Spanish word for gold. Some gold panning continues to produce limited amounts of the precious metal in the northern Costa rivers.

Ancient mines in El Oro Province have produced gold since 1549. Mining still continues. Silver is found in the same mines.

Deposits of iron, copper, and zinc have been located. Marble, gypsum, limestone, and coal are also mined. Unfortunately, much of Ecuador's mineral deposits are in inaccessible regions.

POTENTIAL

Ecuador's resources are many. However, the country is troubled with extensive loans, with vast areas still recovering from El Niño in 1982-83, and with social problems. The worldwide recession in the late 1970s and early 1980s decreased the demand for the country's natural resources.

The Inca ruled much of what is now Ecuador in the late 1400s. Ingapirca (above), near Cuenca, has artifacts and ruins of the Inca. Below is an Inca gold mask.

Chapter 3

THE FIRST INHABITANTS IN ECUADOR PREHISTORY

The first inhabitants of Ecuador may have come down through North and Central America to South America. Some scholars instead claim they may have been Polynesian, arriving by boat from islands far away in the Pacific Ocean.

Near Quito, high in the Andes, stone tools and flake knives have been found. They date from 9000 B.C. The oldest ceramics that have been discovered were made about 3200 B.C. They are similar to ancient Japanese ceramics.

The country's prehistory is hard to reconstruct. The first conquistadores destroyed much of the culture of the people they conquered.

Few archaeological excavations have been undertaken. The earliest remains of the first farmers in the highlands have been dated at 1000 B.C. These are the Monjashuaico ruins in the province of Azuay.

The most advanced culture was found in the provinces of Esmeraldas and Manabí along the coast. In Manabí simple statues

Gold ornaments and headdresses of the Inca

and U-shaped seats resting on pedestals have been found. The pedestals represented crouching animals or human figures.

In Esmeraldas stone sculptured heads that resemble those of the Maya in Mexico have been unearthed. In museums in Quito, Guayaquil, and Cuenca are exhibited ceramics, items in gold, and weavings that have retained their beautiful colors.

PRE-INCAN HISTORY

Two nations were formed in the century before Incan invasion. The one in the highlands (Sierra) was the Quitus nation. Along the coastland were the Caras with their king, Shyri.

When these two nations were joined, the strong Shyris nation was rivaled in the south by the Puruha Indian tribe. The Puruhas lived in what is now Chimborazo Province. Some of the descendants of their rulers, the Duchicela caste, live in Guayaquil even now.

A bitter war erupted between the Shyris and the Puruhas. Finally, peace was achieved when the daughter of King Caran Shyri married the son of Condorazo (Big Condor), a Duchicela chief.

A descendant, Atauqui Duchicela Shyri XIII, was king when the Inca invaded land to the north of Peru. This occurred sometime between 1455 and 1460.

THE INCA

The ancient Aymara and Quechua nations founded a state in Cuzco (Quechua), Peru, around 1200. The language they spoke, which later was spoken throughout the Andes, was Quechua. These Inca were governed by a king who was also the high priest of the sun god Inti. He was the Sapay Inca.

In time the Inca became the rulers of Peru, Bolivia, and parts of Chile and Argentina. They called their state the Tahuantinsuyo, empire of the four quarters of the world.

Then the Inca started north. They met resistance from the Cañaris of the southern Sierras. The Cañaris and Palta tribes were separated from the Quitus and Puruha tribes by the high Andean peaks. The Cañaris fought bravely, defeating the Inca in some battles.

Finally, the Cañaris surrendered to the Inca king, Tupac-Yupanqui. The king built a fortress where Cuenca is located today. But he chose to return to Cuzco, the golden city, following the birth of his son, Huayna-Capac.

Later, Tupac-Yupanqui decided to conquer the Shyris in Quito.

Indians called Quito their capital before the Inca captured it in the late 1400s.

Hualcopo Duchicela Shyri XIV was the successor to Atauqui. He and his men fought bravely. It took twelve years for the Inca to conquer the Shyris in the northern territories and their stronghold at Quito. Huayna-Capac drove his armies north into what is now Colombia.

The Shyri King Hualcopo, against the will of some of his war chiefs, sought peace. Defeated and tired, Hualcopo was succeeded by his son Cacha, who joined the war chiefs near Otavalo for a last battle with the Inca under Huayna-Capac, son of Tupac-Yupanqui. Cacha was defeated.

To bring peace at last, Huayna-Capac married Paccha, daughter of the rival king. Their son, Atahualpa, was the last of the Inca sovereigns.

Huayna-Capac lived in Quito for thirty years. He left his vast empire at his death in 1526 to his two sons, Huascar and Atahualpa. Huascar, his son by an earlier marriage, was born in Cuzco. So Huayna-Capac decreed that the southern part of the empire with Cuzco as its capital be ruled by Huascar.

Atahualpa, the last of the Inca kings, died in 1533.

Atahualpa was born in Quito. Huayna-Capac assigned the northern part of the empire to Atahualpa, with its capital at Quito.

In a short time, war broke out between the two half brothers and their followers. Atahualpa and his troops moved south into Peru. They defeated Huascar at Cajamarca. Huascar was taken prisoner and later assassinated.

Atahualpa continued on until his forces conquered Cuzco in 1530. The empire was reunited under one ruler. His military successes earned Atahualpa the title the "First Ecuadorian."

But the empire was not to continue for many more years.

DISCOVERY AND CONQUEST

The Inca used forced labor to have the Indians build roads to every corner of the empire. Over them moved food and other supplies. Threats of revolt could quickly be met with fresh troops traveling over the same roads. Especially important was the road between Cuzco, Peru, and Quito, Ecuador.

Francisco Pizarro conquered the Inca and made it possible for Spain to colonize much of South America.

Nevertheless, the Inca's vast resources assured the Indians of a food supply in times of crop failures. But Indian tribes like the Cañaris deeply resented Inca rule.

By the beginning of the sixteenth century, Spaniards in Panama had heard tales of a rich kingdom in the south. Expeditions were sent out from Panama to find it.

One of these explorers was Vasco Núñez de Balboa, the first European to discover the Pacific Ocean. Other explorers went down as far as present-day Colombia. But the rich kingdom was not there.

Then Francisco Pizarro led an expedition down the coast of South America in search of Biru, the name given to the Inca kingdom.

The Spaniards sailed along the coast of Ecuador, crossing the equator. As they neared Peru they found Indians with gold and jewels. These were what they were seeking.

The Inca Empire must be conquered.

THE SPANIARDS REACH PERU

Near Cajamarca in northern Peru, the Spaniards went ashore. There were scarcely more than two hundred conquistadores in the party.

Pizarro invited Atahualpa to a meeting in the town square. Instead, the Spaniards took him prisoner, demanding a ransom for his release. The Inca brought several tons of gold for the ransom.

Pizarro and his men took the gold. Then they executed Atahualpa. The date was August 29, 1533. The Inca said, "The sun became dark at midday." Their rulers had always been considered high priests of the sun god. Only seven years had passed since Huayna-Capac had died and his sons had become Inca rulers.

How could two hundred men conquer the proud Inca? They wore suits of chain mail and carried firearms. They rode horses—which the Indians had never seen. Besides, there had been rivalry between the two leaders. Inca authority had decreased.

QUITO FALLS

Quito, however, still remained under Inca control. The Spaniards were in Peru. Aided by the Cañaris, the Spaniards fought their way north to Quito by the middle of 1534. The Inca general Rumiñahui destroyed the city before retreating. He died in a final battle with the Spaniards.

Sebastián de Benalcázar was the officer in charge of the Spanish

In conquering the Inca, Benalcázar's men razed Quito in 1534. The Spanish rebuilt the city, and many red-roofed colonial buildings still remain.

troops and Cañaris Indians when they reached Quito. On the ruins, he founded the town of San Francisco de Quito on December 6, 1534.

He established a municipal government when Quito was rebuilt. Then he built Guayaquil on the coast as a port for Quito. A road connecting the two cities was constructed. He ended the Indian guerrilla warfare and completed the conquest of Ecuador.

His successors heard of gold to the east. In 1541 Gonzalo Pizarro set out from Quito with an expedition to find gold.

Supplies for the soldiers and their Indian guides ran out. Pizarro sent Francisco de Orellana with a small force down the Napo River in search of food.

Orellana did not return. Instead he and his men went down the Napo and on into the Amazon. Many months later they reached the Atlantic Ocean. They were the first Europeans to see and travel on the Amazon.

Gonzalo Pizarro returned to Quito in June, 1542. He learned that his brother, Francisco, had been killed in Lima, Peru. The Spanish colony in Peru and Ecuador was in turmoil for ten years.

In 1542 the Spanish crown had established the New Laws. There were many people who felt that the Indians were mistreated. The New Laws put restrictions on the treatment of the Indians. Many of the conquistadores lost title to their Indian workers. Then the Spaniards revolted against the viceroys sent to govern the colony.

After 1548, Quito was peaceful. The Spaniards built beautiful churches in the city. A government palace was constructed. Except for earthquakes in the highlands or an occasional volcanic eruption, the time was fairly peaceful. But life for the Indians was still difficult.

San Francisco Church, the oldest church in South America, was founded in 1535 and is considered one of the world's masterpieces of baroque art. The interior of La Campañía Church is covered with gold leaf.

Chapter 4

A TUMULTUOUS HISTORY

Ecuador as a country did not exist after the Spanish conquest. It was linked with what are now Colombia and Peru. The chief administrative offices were in Lima.

COLONIAL PERIOD

After 1548, order was restored in Quito. Aside from earthquakes in the highlands, fires, and epidemics, the country was fairly peaceful for almost two centuries. This has been called the good colonial time.

Religious orders built monasteries and churches. Other Spanish-style buildings were erected.

The region was a province under the viceroyalty of Nueva Castilla (Peru). In 1563 Quito's population consisted of one thousand Spanish men, two hundred Spanish women, and perhaps ten thousand Indians. From this originated Ecuador's *mestizos*, persons of mixed Spanish and Indian ancestry. Hispanic traditions replaced native culture in many parts of daily life.

The Franciscan order in the Roman Catholic church recognized the artistic talent of the Indians. They opened a school soon after their arrival to incorporate these skills into Spanish arts.

Some of the land that the native population had farmed was taken over by Spaniards. It was also granted to the church.

Indians were forced to work the land for the Spaniards who were to supervise them. In theory the land belonged to Spain. The Spaniards were expected to provide proper supervision of the Indians. Instead, the Indians were often badly treated and lacked proper food. Many Indians were forced to work in the mines.

Dissatisfaction arose over long administrative delays caused by the long distance between Lima and Quito. In 1563 the *Audiencia* of Quito was granted the right to deal directly with the Council of the Indies. The *Audiencia* was a large territory extending into what are now Colombia and Peru. It stretched from the Pacific Ocean to explored areas in the Amazon.

Trade was conducted through Spain. Everything imported or exported in the *Audiencia* had to pass through Seville or Cadiz, Spain. Trade between Spain's Western Hemisphere colonies was prohibited. However, Guayaquil was sometimes exempt. This was to repay the city for its losses through fires and pirate invasions. Guayaquil thus became an important port. It was also a shipbuilding center for the west coast of South America.

There were few Indians in the Costa. Negro slaves were brought from the Caribbean to work the plantations. The cultivation of crops and the care of livestock in the Sierra was done by Indians. On the coast it was done by Negro slave labor. New crops were introduced.

COLONIAL CHANGE

Changes in government took place in the Americas. The *Audiencia* of Quito was transferred from the viceroyalty of Lima to the viceroyalty of New Granada in 1739. This new viceroyalty had its capital at Santa Fé de Bogotá in what is now Colombia.

Spain's grip on shipping regulations was relaxed. Visitors from other countries brought new ideas. Wealthy Spaniards in Ecuador sent their sons to Europe to study. Printed matter from other countries, which had been restricted, now circulated.

The colonial system continued in its oppression of the Indians. *Criollos* (Creoles), Spaniards born in America, were firmly in control together with the church.

Quietly the Indians endured their suffering. But the seeds of discontent were soon to erupt.

Toward the close of the eighteenth century there were several Indian uprisings in the Sierra and on the coast. The problems of the Indians were shared by *mestizos,* whose status was very little better than their own.

In the uprisings property was destroyed. Many *Criollos* and Spaniards lost their lives. The Indians were finally subdued.

But there was also discontent among the *Criollos.* Spanish trade restrictions, unfair laws, and news of independence movements in other countries motivated them.

Discontent and resentment against Spain was growing in other parts of South America as well. There were many who yearned for independence.

VOICES FOR INDEPENDENCE

Francisco Eugenio de Santa Cruz y Espejo was born in Quito in 1747. His father was Indian. Although he was of mixed parentage, he obtained a university education. He became a doctor and a gifted writer.

As editor of the first periodical during the colonial period, he influenced many with his thinking. He sought complete independence from Spain and the establishment of a democracy.

Espejo was arrested for his critical attacks on the colonial rule. He died in prison in 1795. He did not live to see independence. But his ideals of liberty and justice paved the way for the country's future independence.

Another writer voicing the call for independence was José Joaquín Olmedo. As a poet he achieved fame not only in his own country but throughout South America.

Olmedo met Simón Bolívar, for whom he had great admiration. Bolívar was a great northern independence leader.

THE REPUBLICAN PERIOD BEGINS

Juan Pío Montúfar, a friend of Espejo, led *Criollo* patriots in Quito in a cry for independence. The date was August 10, 1809, still celebrated as a national holiday.

Spain had been invaded by Napoleon of France. In 1808 King Charles IV of Spain had abdicated. His son, Ferdinand VII, assumed the throne, but Napoleon placed him in confinement. News of these affairs soon reached Quito. The time seemed right for Montúfar and the patriots.

In December, 1811, a congress declared complete independence and established the state of Quito, which included the entire *Audiencia.* In February, 1812, a constitution was drafted and approved.

For a time Spain had considered granting its colonies in South America a form of independence under a commonwealth status. The colonies would have local autonomy but would still be united to Spain. But when the plan did not take place, colonial rule became stricter than before.

Left: Simón Bolívar is called the Liberator of South America.
Right: A statue of Antonio José de Sucre, Bolívar's field marshal

By 1820, the three countries now called Ecuador, Colombia, and Venezuela united to fight for independence. Their leader was Simón Bolívar.

On October 9, 1820, Guayaquil set up a government council, declaring its independence from the *Audiencia*. Young patriots and some of the local troops sought to carry the struggle to other parts of the *Audiencia*.

Leaders of independence in other parts of South America came to their aid—Simón Bolívar from Venezuela, José de San Martín from Argentina, and Bolívar's leading lieutenant, Antonio José de Sucre.

On May 24, 1822, Field Marshal Sucre led revolutionary forces down to Quito. On the slopes of Mount Pichincha they defeated the Spanish royalists. Sucre is honored for gaining Ecuador's independence, and the nation's currency is named for him.

San Martín favored having Guayaquil join Peru. Bolívar hoped that what are now Ecuador, Venezuela, Colombia, and Panama would unite into one country. The four countries, what had been the viceroyalty of New Granada, would obtain independence together. Simón Bolívar hoped eventually to see a United States of South America.

GRAN COLOMBIA

In 1822, Ecuador joined the Federation of Gran Colombia. That same year a congress, called in Guayaquil, voted the city should become a part of the federation.

Bolívar became president of Gran Colombia. The seat of government remained in Bogotá, Colombia.

Simón Bolívar led Gran Colombia in the war for the liberation of Peru after San Martín's resignation in 1822. Ecuador was closest to the battlefields. It suffered greatly from the fighting. In 1825 the war ended.

Then in 1828 Peru and Gran Colombia fought in a border dispute. From the sea Guayaquil was bombarded and the city destroyed. At the Battle of Tarqui, General Juan José Flores and the Ecuadorians defeated the Peruvians in February, 1829.

In 1830, eight years after its founding, Gran Colombia was dissolved. The three parts became separate republics: Colombia, Venezuela, and Ecuador. (Panama broke away later.)

In Quito representatives voted to thank Bolívar for his contribution to Ecuador's independence. Later that year an assembly drew up a constitution.

ATTEMPTS AT DEMOCRACY

The constitution provided for three branches of government: executive, legislative, and judicial. The president, elected for a four-year term, had to be an Ecuadorian citizen.

A clause in the constitution provided citizenship for anyone who had fought in Ecuador's independence. General Flores, who had been a Venezuelan, was easily elected.

The country was in serious financial difficulty. It owed a large percentage of the war debt in the fight against Peru.

When General Flores realized he could not be reelected in 1834, he supported Vicente Rocafuerte, previously an independence leader.

When Rocafuerte became president, Flores remained as commander general of the army. In five years he returned to power. In 1843, a Flores-controlled congress prepared a new constitution. It became known as the Charter of Slavery. Flores had tired of democracy.

The March, 1845 revolution ended Flores's rule. A government council was set up in Guayaquil. It challenged the central government in Quito.

The country remained in confusion for many years. In 1860 Gabriel García Moreno became *jefe supremo* (dictator). He served as president from 1861 to 1865 and 1869 to 1875. He began construction of a road and a railroad between Quito and Guayaquil. He was a supporter of the church. Compulsory education was introduced but was difficult to enforce without sufficient schools and teachers. The Indians remained in a deplorable condition.

The struggle between the conservative and liberal forces

continued. In the liberal movement Juan Montalvo, a talented writer, became a leader. He was forced into exile in Colombia.

On August 6, 1875, García Moreno was assassinated on the steps of the Government Palace. Ecuador's problems were far from over.

MANY LEADERS, MANY CONSTITUTIONS

In the years that followed, many men assumed the presidency. In the first 133 years of independence, the leadership changed sixty-seven times. At one time there were four presidents in twenty-six days. Some made notable contributions. General Eloy Alfaro, president from 1895 to 1901 and 1906 to 1911, improved the educational system. The railroad between Quito and Guayaquil was completed. Unfortunately, there was no land reform, and the Indians remained extremely poor.

When Alfaro was driven from office in 1911, he was sent into exile. When he returned, he was murdered in Quito in 1912.

With his successor, General Leonidas Plaza, Alfaro had been responsible for reforms. The separation of church and state, confiscation of large church estates that were then to be administered by the state, freedom of thought, and educational improvements were some of their contributions.

Through the years, the country seemed to go from one civil war to another. When Guillermo Franco felt that it would be safer to have Guayaquil and southern Ecuador under Peruvian rule, the other cities forgot some of their differences. They united to thwart Franco's plans.

The country had endured leaders who might be considered tyrants. Some who were elected president arranged for a successor to be elected following their term of office. Then it was understood the first man would resume power. Dishonest elections were common.

So unstable was the government at times that in 1944, when José María Velasco Ibarra was deposed by the military, there were three more presidents in less than a year.

LAND GRAB

Ecuador lost large areas of its country to Colombia and Brazil early in the twentieth century. In 1935 Colombia ceded to Peru land claimed by Ecuador. By 1941 Peru invaded an area in the Oriente.

To establish peace in the hemisphere, the United States and Mexico called for a meeting of the foreign ministers of South America. This was a crucial time. World War II had begun and peace in South America was important.

The foreign ministers voted to allow Peru to retain the land. Uprisings broke out in Guayaquil and Riobamba at the decision. Maps of Ecuador today show this large area as still claimed by the country. On a border town on the Amazon, there are garrisons stationed to prevent further confrontation.

STABILITY

By 1948, when Galo Plaza Lasso was elected president, a period of stability ensued. Economic progress, increased agricultural productivity, and foreign exports marked his four years in office.

It was not until April, 1979 that a complete return to democracy took place. Free elections were held. A lawyer, Jaime Roldós

León Febres Cordero became president of Ecuador in 1984.

Aguilera, became president. When he and his wife and other members of the government were killed in a plane crash on May 24, 1981, Vice-president Osvaldo Hurtado became president. The legislative assembly elected León Roldós Aguilera, the deceased president's brother, to be vice-president.

On August 10, 1984, León Febres Cordero was inaugurated as president. He had won a runoff election in May. It was the first time in twenty-four years that control in Ecuador passed from one constitutionally elected government to another.

The new president faced tremendous problems. Ecuador needed 77 percent of its export income to meet its foreign debt obligations. Unemployment and underemployment were high. So was inflation. There was great need for housing.

Ecuador's tumultuous history is gradually finding a calmer solution to its problems. Cooperation between all of the countries in the Americas is essential. It is the way for Ecuador—and the other South American countries—to solve their great economic problems.

GOVERNMENT

Although Ecuador was a democracy for many years, there were times when it became a dictatorship. The military assumed control in 1972, for example, when it deposed the duly-elected president.

Military officers replaced civilian governors in the provinces. The legislature had been dissolved in 1970 under President José María Velasco Ibarra. The military did not restore it.

Between 1812 and 1967 eighteen constitutions were written, two of them prior to the country's independence. Twice the government discarded a constitution and returned to a previous one.

In 1970 President Velasco Ibarra ruled that the constitution of 1967 was void. He returned to the one written in 1946. The military junta that deposed him reactivated the constitution of 1945.

Since 1830 all of the constitutions have provided for a presidential rather than a parliamentary system. There are executive, legislative, and judicial branches.

Ecuadorian constitutions have been based on the United States document and on French declarations of human rights. The legislature has generally consisted of two houses, a senate, and a chamber of deputies. Today the legislative branch is unicameral (having one house) with sixty-nine elected members.

Ecuadorians have become increasingly interested in their government. There has been a steady increase in the number of registered voters. From 1948 to 1960 there was a rather stable constitutional rule.

The country is divided into twenty provinces. Each province is divided into cantons, or municipalities, and parishes. Previously the governors, political chiefs of the cantons, and the political lieutenants of the parishes were appointed by the president. The 1945 constitution provided for national, provincial, and parish elections. The military junta rejected this as inoperative.

After nine years of dictatorship, the country returned to civilian rule on August 10, 1979, with the election of Jaime Roldós as president. All citizens eighteen and over have the right to vote.

The president appoints the governors of the provinces. Canton and city officials are elected.

The president, vice-president, and the legislature are elected for a five-year term. The vice-president is head of the National Development Council, which is in charge of economic planning.

Only those candidates belonging to a recognized political party may run for office. There are twelve different legal parties. At the close of 1981, for example, no party held more than twelve seats in the congress.

The president also selects twelve ministers for cabinet positions. The Government Palace, Congress Palace, the Supreme Court of Justice, and the offices of the cabinet ministers are located in the republic's capital, Quito.

President León Febres Cordero gave his inaugural address on August 10, 1984. He declared war on terrorism, drug trafficking and use, unemployment, and the huge foreign debt.

The provinces, nineteen on the mainland and one for the Galápagos, have elected councils that are responsible for public services, coordinating the activities of the municipality, and the promotion of overall development.

Municipal or canton administrations are governed by elected councils of fifteen councillors or aldermen. The councils are presided over by elected mayors. Municipalities collect taxes to provide the many services required by the town or city.

Judges of the Supreme Court of Justice supervise the Superior Courts and the lower courts. The Supreme Court handles both civil and criminal cases.

Because they deal with tourists, many policemen have received training in the history, folklore, art, and geography of Ecuador.

NATIONAL DEFENSE

The republic's armed forces include about thirty thousand in the army and five thousand each in the navy and in the air force. Both the army and the air force have academies for officer training near Quito. The naval academy and the air force flying school are at Salinas.

Branches of the armed forces have contributed much through civic action programs. Road construction, well digging, school construction, the teaching of literacy courses, providing medical and dental services, and reforestation projects all have been undertaken. Artillery and cavalry units in Quito have brought children from Guayaquil for a month of sports activities. All of these programs have brought the military into high regard with some citizens.

The National Civil Police safeguards the security of citizens and their possessions, maintains peace and order throughout the country, investigates crimes, and arrests violators of the law. Civil police are trained at the police academy for three years after high school graduation.

Urban and rural police also are present to maintain order and prevent crime. Since urban police come in contact with tourists, they have been trained in history, forklore, art, and geography. They have also been given courses in English.

Traffic police are a division of the National Civil Police. Vehicles are checked, traffic accidents are investigated, and traffic control is afforded. Guayaquil has the greatest number of traffic accidents.

WORLD WAR II

Ecuador declared war on Japan immediately after the bombing of Pearl Harbor on December 7, 1941. The United States was granted permission to construct an air base on the island of Baltra in the Galápagos. American planes flew reconnaissance flights to the Panama Canal for defense in the event of a Japanese attack. Later, the United States offered to buy the island, but Ecuador declined to sell. The airstrip on Baltra is still in use for commercial flights.

BORDER DISPUTES

The boundary between Ecuador and Peru supposedly had been established in 1563. The boundary separated the *audiencias* of Lima and Quito. A dispute arose between the two countries over the right to that territory.

Many Peruvians moved into the disputed territory in the nineteenth and twentieth centuries. Soon they outnumbered the Ecuadorians. The region is a great rain forest between the Putumayo and Amazon rivers.

A treaty in 1890 divided the disputed territory in half. Ecuador then had an outlet on the Marañón River. Farther downstream the Marañón becomes the Amazon. But Ecuador rejected the treaty in 1894 because it gave no direct access to the Amazon.

A decision in arbitration by the king of Spain gave Ecuador even less territory. The boundary dispute was not settled.

Every few years Ecuadorian military garrisons challenged the Peruvians. Talks between the two countries in Washington, D.C., ended in 1938 without resolving the problem.

Then in May, 1941, the United States, Brazil, and Argentina offered to mediate the dispute. But Peru refused to meet. By July fighting broke out. It ended when the three mediating countries ordered a cease-fire.

The Protocol of Rio de Janeiro, signed on January 29, 1942, awarded 70,000 square miles (181,299 square kilometers) of the disputed territory to Peru. But the boundary dispute was not settled. The treaty's description of the terrain did not match the physical features of the land. Forty-nine miles (78 kilometers) of border remain undemarcated. Ecuador has refused to recognize the portion that is correctly demarcated.

Armed hostilities broke out again in January, 1981, along the undemarcated section of the border. Ecuador has appealed to the United Nations and to the Organization of American States to settle the border question. Toward the end of 1981 neither of the opposing countries wanted to resume hostilities. But Ecuador still hopes to obtain the disputed area and gain access to the Marañón River.

Relations with the other two nations in the former Gran Colombia—Colombia and Venezuela—have been cordial. However, in 1935 Colombia ceded Ecuadorian-claimed territory to Peru. This strained relations between the two countries.

The Otavaleños are an industrious group of Indians who have adapted well to the modern world. Above: Two women talking. Below left: Winnowing wheat. Below right: Craftsman displaying his weaving

Chapter 5

ECUADOR'S MANY PEOPLE

Twenty-five percent of Ecuador's population is Indian. The differences in the groups or tribes come from the great variation in geography.

The Indians of the Sierra, the Costa, and the Oriente still show marked differences in culture.

THE SIERRA INDIANS

Over 1.5 million Indians inhabit the Sierra or highlands. Farms here have been dated from 1000 B.C. The fertile valleys provided independent groups with farming areas that could be defended easily. But there was still an opportunity for contacts between the various groups and also with those in the lowlands.

After the Inca conquered the region, the Quechua language was introduced. When Spanish missionaries adopted the language, it became the language of nearly all of the tribes.

Despite the influence of the Spaniards, who introduced Christianity, there were still tribal differences in housing, mode of dress, religious practices, and medical practices.

The Otavaleños are perhaps the most distinctive tribe today. Living high in the Sierra, they have become expert weavers. Each

Left: Many Otavaleños own their own farms. Right: World-famous woolen goods are displayed in the market at Otavalo.

week they take their crafts to Otavalo, walking many miles to reach the market.

Otavalo sweaters, ponchos, and other woolen goods are eagerly bought by tourists. Otavalo men travel into other northern South American countries to sell their wares. Others travel to Quito on the Pan-American Highway to offer their products.

The Otavaleños have been so industrious and successful that they have been able to purchase land and own small farms.

Their success in commercial weaving has given them a higher standard of living than most other Indians and even *mestizos* and neighboring whites.

Two other important, but smaller, Indian tribes in the highlands are the Salasacas and the Saraguros. The Salasacas have never been tenant farmers. They have always owned their land. Similarly, the Saraguros, with large herds of cattle, have maintained their independence. The Otavaleños, Salasacas, and

Salasacan Indian children (left) singing in a mission school. Saraguros (right) live in the highlands.

the Saraguros are prosperous tribes maintaining their own identity.

The Sierra Indians are rural. Only about 2 percent live in large communities. Most of them subsist on agriculture. Their diet consists of beans, barley, potatoes, corn, and wheat.

Until the Agrarian Reform Law of 1964, most of the Sierra Indians worked as tenant farmers on *haciendas* (large estates). The tenant farmers, called *huasipungueros,* worked several days a week for a *hacienda* owner. They received a small plot to farm for themselves, a home site, and pasturage for a few animals. Their pay was very low. The land they worked was the least desirable.

The Agrarian Reform Law made the land tenancy illegal. Many *huasipungueros* have received title to their land. But their farming methods have improved very little. Oxen and wooden plows are used to prepare the land. Hoes and digging sticks are used on steeper slopes.

A Colorado Indian family goes to the market (left). Colorado men put red dye on their body and hair.

Despite some changes that have improved conditions for the Indians, they remain submissive. They avoid unnecessary contact with white or *mestizo* society. They have a traditional fear and distrust of all outsiders.

Since the arrival of Spaniards, the Roman Catholic church has been influential in the Indians' lives. Although most Indians are Catholic, they retain their ancient folk beliefs. Spirits are felt to govern natural forces. So they believe health, the weather, and the success of their crops depend on these spirits.

Catholic priests are shown great respect. Fiestas, six to twelve a year, are important in the social life of the community. Religious rituals, including baptism, marriage, and funerals, are meaningful ceremonies for the Indians.

THE COSTA INDIANS

Only two small tribes indigenous to the Costa remain. They are the Colorado and Cayapa.

A Colorado Indian boy makes a paste from the achiote nut and applies the dye to his hair.

Neither tribe has a traditional village. They are hunters and fishermen as well as farmers.

The Colorados are named for the red body paint made from the seed of the annatto tree. The men cut their hair at ear length, part it in the middle, and have bangs. Then they plaster it with the same dye as the body paint.

The women wear their hair long and uncovered. They use the red dye on their faces only. Their skirts are wraparound and knee length.

Today some of the Colorados' income comes from posing for tourist pictures in the village of Santo Domingo de los Colorados. They have become efficient farmers. Their bananas are sent to the national market.

The Cayapas now settle along the Cayapas River, where they have herds of cattle. They, too, raise bananas. Some of their income comes from rubber and their traditional handicrafts.

Other Indian groups have moved into the Costa. The Coayqueres have moved south from Colombia. Yumbos have

Auca Indians splitting vines to use for weaving baskets.

moved in from the Oriente. A few Sierra Indians have come seeking a better life.

Other Costa groups have become *montuvios. Montuvios* are fishermen, peasants, and plantation workers often of mixed racial backgrounds. Generally, they are considered to be at least part Indian. They have had contact with whites for several centuries.

THE ORIENTE INDIANS

Many of the Indians of the Oriente also have had contact with whites for many years. Most of these were missionaries and traders who came for the raw materials the Indians gathered in the jungle.

With the discovery of oil in the Oriente, new roads are being constructed. Many people are moving in. The culture of the Indians who remain in the Oriente is threatened.

The remaining tribes include the Yumbos, Zaparos, Jívaros, and

Left: An Auca Indian woman eating fruit. Right: Auca children in a classroom

Aucas. Some have moved deeper into the jungle to escape the intrusion into their land.

The Yumbos came from many smaller groups after the Spanish conquest. They adopted the Quechua language and lost their own tribal cultures.

The Yumbos are farmers. But, since the land they clear soon wears out, they must move frequently. Their houses are constructed of bamboo with grass thatched roofs.

They raise yucca and plantain. Their *naranjilla* crop, a small orange, is sold to truckers. Some of the men work on coffee plantations.

They are Roman Catholics but hold, also, to some of their old beliefs. Like other Indians, they remain aloof from whites.

The Jívaros are divided into seventy-five groups. They live near the Peruvian border. They are primarily hunters but also raise some crops. Unlike other forest Indians, they raise domestic animals, chickens, a few cattle, and guinea pigs, which are a favorite in the Indian diet in many parts of the country.

The women make ceramics and the men do the spinning and weaving. For many years they were feared for their hostility to intruders. In their intergroup warfare, they often beheaded their enemies. These human heads were shrunk and thought to have magical powers. The government has banned the sale of shrunken heads *(tzantzas)*.

INDIAN INTEGRATION

Many international agencies have assisted the government in integrating the Indians into Ecuadorian society. Unfortunately, many of the programs provided by outside agencies are based on Western rather than Indian values. The programs also suffer from the Indians' distrust of outsiders.

Radio has been used with some success in teaching the Indians better health and sanitation methods.

THE *MESTIZOS*

In the most recent census, 55 percent of the population was classed as *mestizo*. *Mestizos* are generally considered to be persons of Spanish-Indian ancestry or culture. They share in the national culture but are influenced by Indian traditions.

In the Sierra the *mestizo* may own small areas. Some may still work as *huasipungueros*, working for an owner in exchange for a small plot of ground.

Mestizos, generally, are better off than the Indians. Although they may live in poverty, they often vote and can aspire to a better life.

In the cities, where young *mestizos* may go, they find some

Indians and blacks face racial and economic barriers in Ecuador.

employment as manual laborers. Many lack sufficient education to enable them to achieve higher status.

The cities in the Costa, where many go, do not offer enough opportunities for employment. Some return to the Sierra.

MINORITIES

Blacks account for 10 percent of the total population. They live primarily in the coastal region. They were imported to work on the coastal sugar plantations in the sixteenth century and later. In 1852, when slavery was abolished in Ecuador, there were about eight thousand Negroes in the country.

Today, the population includes mulattoes as well as those of unmixed race. Many of them work in the fishing industry on shrimp and cargo boats. But many more are employed in agriculture. Few, however, own land. Most families keep a few pigs and goats.

The status of the Negro or African is higher than that of the Indian, but he faces racial and economic barriers.

In the port city of Guayaquil there is a concentration of Lebanese. They are generally merchants.

Chinese have also settled along the coast. They, too, are shopkeepers. The Chinese community is north of Guayaquil in the town of Quevedo.

At times, Ecuador has tried to attract other immigrants. There are families who have come from Germany, France, England, and Ireland.

THE HISPANICS

For 450 years, Ecuador has been under Hispanic domination. From the small band of conquistadores to today's 10 percent of the population, persons of Spanish heritage have maintained authority.

A rivalry between the Hispanics of the Sierra and those of the Costa developed. But the pattern of Ecuadorian society in both regions was based on Spanish heritage. The language, land ownership, and religion had come from Spain. Nevertheless, the upper classes of the Sierra and Costa are different.

Economic and political power, educational opportunities, and status in society became the right of a minority who traced their heritage to Spain. This small minority forms the elite of Ecuador. The present elite in the Costa did not form until three hundred years after that in the Sierra.

THE MIDDLE CLASSES

But there were other whites whose status did not match this elite. By 1950 a small middle-class society developed. These are

Housing for the middle class in Quito

educated people. Many are businessmen and professionals, army officers, and government employees. To be considered middle class, a person must have at least a secondary education, perform no manual labor, and have appropriate dress and manners.

Even the middle class is divided into two classes. The lower-middle-class members may have small businesses or teach in primary schools. Upper-middle-class persons are the executives and well-to-do professionals.

The Hispanics, often called "whites," put great emphasis on their Spanish heritage. They are found mostly in the large cities of Quito, Guayaquil, Cuenca, Ambato, and Riobamba.

In the smaller towns, *mestizos* often hold positions of the same importance as those of whites in the city. Like the whites, the *mestizo* is Spanish speaking and often has the same values, mode of dress, and attitudes.

The elite of the Sierra has tried to maintain control over the country. The Costa has grown stronger and has challenged the central government. The two groups feel they have different economic needs. They also differ in their attitudes toward national institutions, especially the Catholic church.

Above: The Pan-American Highway runs north to south through Ecuador.
Below: Manta, a small port on the Pacific Ocean, has shrimp beds off the coast.

Chapter 6

LIVING, LEARNING, AND WORKING

CITIES AND TOWNS, *HACIENDAS* AND PLANTATIONS

Most of Ecuador's roads were built in the last forty years. One of the most important is the Pan-American Highway, which crosses the country from north to south, from Colombia to Peru.

Towns and cities have been built along the country's 12,000 miles (19,312 kilometers) of roads. Many towns grew up along waterways. *Haciendas* and plantations now have access to cities.

Santo Domingo de los Colorados is a major junction for several highways. From there, roads lead to Quito, Esmeraldas, Manta, and Guayaquil. It is predicted that by the year 2000, the town will have a population of half a million.

INTERNAL MIGRATION

The government has attempted to resettle families in suitable locations. The largest resettlement has taken place at Santo Domingo de los Colorados on the western slopes of the Andes.

Left: Harvesting bananas on a plantation in the Costa near the Peruvian border. A good portion of the bananas are exported, but some are sold locally (right).

The institute responsible for the program now has field offices in the settlement areas to help people obtain title to the land.

About 40 percent of the population lives in urban areas. Pichincha Province, in which Quito is located, is the only Sierra province in which population has increased. Internal migration has reduced the population elsewhere in the highlands.

Thousands of people have migrated from the Sierra to the Costa. Some moved to the towns and cities. Others, accustomed to rural life, settled in rural areas in the northern province of Esmeraldas. The population in the Costa has increased rapidly.

Not all migration was to towns and cities, however. As the number of banana plantations increased, subsistence farmers in the Sierra moved down to El Oro Province. They came from the adjacent provinces of Loja and Azuay.

It was difficult for those in rural areas to leave their homes and move to towns or cities. They had little, if any, education. They

This house would be classified as a villa.

had no money. They also knew that their social status was inferior. But often in desperation they made the move.

Those who moved from small towns in the Costa to cities had an easier adjustment.

Within the last ten years, a colonization program was developed for the Oriente. Spontaneous settlers had moved into the vicinity of Lake Agrio in Napo Province after the discovery of oil. When they had lived on land for three years, they were able to obtain title to it.

HOUSING

About 50 percent of Ecuador's housing units are classed as *casas* (houses) or *villas* (houses with gardens). They are constructed of permanent materials—brick, stone, concrete, or frame (wood).

The other 50 percent is made of adobe, reed or cane, wattle and daub, or scrap materials. Often the floors are dirt. Cane and reed houses are found primarily in the Costa. Often they are built on

Above: Modern and old buildings are intermingled in Quito.
Below: Huts in Tierra Fría, a mountain town southwest of Riobamba

stilts to prevent flooding during the rainy season. The roofing material is thatch.

In the small towns in the Sierra, two-story adobe houses are more common. The roofs may be of tile.

On the outskirts of the cities, those who have migrated from other regions often build their dwellings of scrap materials. In Guayaquil, for example, they have built in the swampy area around the city. At first, attempts were made to drain the swamps. Now a landfill program has been undertaken.

Guayaquil has been destroyed by fire and earthquake in the past. Many of its frame or wooden buildings were ravaged by termites. Today, construction must conform to building codes. This provides for fire- and earthquake-resistant buildings.

In the working-class neighborhoods of Quito the houses are of adobe with tile roofs. Colonial (Spanish) homes were built of volcanic stone. Elaborate grillwork decorates some houses. The fashionable section of La Ronda is located in the inner city.

New structures in Quito must also be earthquake resistant. But, like Guayaquil, the city has its slums. Many of these substandard houses, often built of scrap materials, are the result of a housing shortage. In the suburbs of Quito modern apartment buildings have been constructed to alleviate this shortage.

In the Indian villages of the Sierra, houses are often no more than one room. The walls are mud and the roof is thatch. Electricity and indoor plumbing are usually lacking. There may be no windows. Sometimes the room may be shared with domestic animals to shelter them from rain.

With a rapidly increasing population, internal migration, and inadequate dwellings throughout the country, there is a great need for more housing.

Central University in Quito is a modern campus.

EDUCATION

Government statistics state that there is an 85 percent literacy rate. There are, however, many people who have had little or no opportunity for education.

Schools were originally opened by the Catholic church. They were attended by children of the Spanish elite. Some schools were opened to teach Indian children arts and handicrafts as well as some reading and writing.

Public education began toward the end of the colonial period. Then, late in the nineteenth century, free primary schools were opened.

In the 1960s, most schools were still in the cities. In other sections of the country, there were few schools that the Quechua-speaking Indians or *mestizos* could attend. Finally, in the 1970s, classes in Quechua were introduced in the primary grades.

Classes are usually large in primary schools.

Education is compulsory and free between six and fourteen years of age. There are many children, however, who are unable to attend school because of distance or family demands.

The Ministry of Education reports that over 1,500,000 children are enrolled in elementary schools. There are about 600,000 in secondary schools and approximately 300,000 in the fourteen universities and seven university-level polytechnical schools. Central, provincial, and municipal governments finance education.

Since the number of schools is still insufficient, many classrooms are used in two sessions each day. Primary children attend in the morning. The afternoon session is for older students. In some cases a third or evening session is arranged for secondary-school students.

Pupils wear uniforms to school. This would seem to make all pupils appear on an equal basis. However, there are many pupils who cannot afford the uniforms.

Many programs have been arranged to provide different opportunities for students in secondary schools. Some students are enrolled in basic studies, others prepare for the university, and others study technical subjects.

Central University in Quito began as San Luis Seminary in 1594. Universities train teachers, doctors, lawyers, engineers, and other professionals. Unfortunately, many professional, technical, and scientific personnel emigrate to other countries, especially the United States. They seek higher salaries and better laboratories, facilities, and libraries than are available in their own country.

WORKING

In the Sierra the labor force is primarily engaged in agriculture, with small plots of land often of poor quality. Farmers do not learn modern farming techniques.

A few Indians have learned trades. Some work part-time as truck drivers or in construction. The women find jobs as domestics, working in the homes of well-to-do families.

Many people are engaged in artisan occupations. These are generally carried on in the home and are done by hand. These handicrafts include items made for home use as well as those for sale in the markets. Ceramics, woven goods, tapestries, rugs, wood carvings, and panama hats are typical.

Those working in the manufacturing sector account for about 17 percent of the gross domestic product. It is intended to supply the domestic market and reduce the amount of imports. Food processing is the most important. Wood products and pharmaceuticals are gaining in importance.

Workers are classified by how they are paid. The *obreros* are blue-collar workers. They are manual laborers who are paid daily or hourly wages. The *empleados* are the white-collar workers who are paid monthly salaries. Some skilled laborers are also *empleados.*

The number of women in the labor force has increased annually. This has been due, in large part, to the migration from rural to urban locations. Many of these women find employment in service jobs in hotels, restaurants, and as servants in private homes.

With increased educational opportunities, many young women are finding jobs in offices.

Children under the age of twelve are not allowed to work. Many children, however, contribute to their family income by selling lottery tickets, herding animals, shining shoes, or doing some odd jobs, especially in the larger cities.

There has been an increasing demand for electricians and other skilled craftsmen. The number of unskilled industrial workers exceeds the number of jobs available. Unemployment is, therefore, high.

THE OTAVALO INDIANS

The Otavalo Indians provide an interesting study of an industrious group high in the Sierra. They are primarily farmers. Many own their own land. Each family's house is set on its own plot of ground rather than in a village. The houses are of mud and wattle with high thatch roofs of *páramo* grass.

The single room is windowless. A door opens out onto a porch where the daily work is done. There may be two kinds of looms on the porch: a Spanish loom and an Indian backstrap.

A millstone for grinding corn each day for porridge may also be

Otavalo Indians spinning wool

on the porch—and a small pen for guinea pigs. The mother will grind the corn and prepare the meals. The father will plow his tiny field or hoe the corn.

When he returns from the field, he will begin work at the loom, weaving a soft wool poncho or material for a woman's skirt. The mother will later make the material into articles of clothing for family use or to take to the market on Saturday. She will also spin wool and cotton yarn. The girls will be taught to spin with the reed spindle, a task they can do even as they make the long journey to market. They will be taught to sew and embroider, to grind corn, and to cook.

Smaller children will take the sheep and the pigs to pasture on the hillsides. Father will teach the boys to farm and how to weave. The older children work with their parents.

The Otavalo family is typical of other Indian families. The nuclear family is very important. There is a very close tie between children and parents and the extended family, close relations who usually live nearby.

THE FAMILY

Both Spanish and Indian traditions stress the importance of close family ties. The man is the head of the household.

In Indian families the parents are more likely to share household and economic activities. Children in upper- and middle-class families have few responsibilities. The boys, as they grow older, are given considerable freedom. Girls, on the other hand, are taught ladylike behavior and are closely supervised.

The extended family or kinship circle is called *parentesco.* It is a source of help in many ways. Among Indian and *mestizo* families the kinship circle may not be as large as in that of the upper- or middle-class family. Among the large landowners and the professionals it provides opportunities for jobs, status, and power.

THE CHURCH

Roman Catholic priests and monks accompanied the conquistadores in their conquest of Ecuador. The church quickly became involved in civil activities. In addition to setting up schools for arts and crafts, the church became the protector of the Indians.

Through the years the church became involved in political activities. It also became the largest single landowner.

In 1895, under the presidency of Eloy Alfaro, the church lost much of its power.

The Indians have converted to Christianity but still retain some of their pagan beliefs. Church attendance is high in the Sierra, especially among the Indians and the upper class. Middle-class and *mestizo* families in the Sierra do not attend quite as regularly.

Left: A woman has prepared a roasted pig. Right: Plátanos *and yuca on sale in a local market.*

The constitution guarantees religious freedom. Since the time of President Alfaro, Protestant missionaries have been permitted to work in the country. Few native-born Ecuadorians have been converted. The Protestants have provided schools and various community services.

NUTRITION

The great differences in the diet of people living in various parts of the country are due to availabilities, preferences, and price.

In the Sierra, the Indian diet is often very bland. Condiments, even salt, may not be used. Fried foods are common. Rice may be fried with onions and herbs. Usually meals are single-dish stews or thick soups. Another favorite is a fried potato cake containing cheese and topped with an egg. It is called a *llapingacho.*

Aji, a hot sauce made with red peppers, tomatoes, onions, and spices, may be used over chicken and rice *(colado)* or other meats. *Humitas,* sweet corn cooked in husks like tamales, are also

Buying hot, tasty potato cakes

favorites. *Empanadas,* wheat pastries filled with meat or cheese, and *sancocho,* made from yucca, meat, and bananas, are frequently served in the Costa.

Poor families have meat on rare occasions. Much-needed protein in the diet is supplied by beans or chick-peas.

Breakfast everywhere may be light, with coffee or tea and bread.

In the cities, lunch may be the principal meal of the day since shops and offices may be closed for two hours. In the major cities, dinner may begin at 7:30 or 8:00 P.M.

Visitors may enjoy trying various typical Ecuadorian dishes. *Plâtanos,* a large fruit similar to bananas, are delicious fried, baked, toasted, or prepared as a cake. Fish soup with green peas, toasted ground peanuts, cheese, and potatoes should be tried.

HEALTH AND SANITATION

Malnutrition continues to be a major problem. Since meat, milk, and eggs are difficult for some families to purchase, children often lack a proper diet.

International and domestic public and private agencies provide free milk and lunch for children through the primary grades. In many areas the National Institute of Nutrition in the Ministry of Social Welfare distributes iodized salt to combat goiter, common where fish is not a regular part of the diet.

Adult education courses are given in some parts of the country to instruct parents in proper nutritional practices.

The Ministry of Public Health is administered through offices in Quito, Guayaquil, Cuenca, and Portoviejo. Malnutrition among infants and children is responsible for lowered resistance to disease. The Ministry, the World Health Organization, and United Nations Children's Fund (UNICEF) combine to work on Ecuador's health problems.

Programs to eradicate yellow fever and smallpox in the Costa were successful. Smallpox vaccinations were given as a preventive measure to almost all children. Cases of malaria have been greatly reduced. Innoculations against polio were administered. Cases of bubonic plague, which had occurred in the Sierra, were reduced by fumigating houses to destroy rats that carry the disease.

Only a small percentage of the doctors and dentists practice in the rural areas. Many emigrate to other countries, primarily the United States.

Mobile units bring health services to suburban and rural areas. Airborne mobile medical and dental emergency services go to the Oriente.

Most of the hospitals were built prior to the turn of the century. In rural areas, the people put great emphasis on home remedies. Among the Highland Indians this includes folklore. Many still believe illness is the result of supernatural causes.

In recent years, however, studies have been conducted on the

Water from a tanker being emptied into a water tank

herbal remedies administered by the Indians. Many have been found to have valuable curative powers. The medical profession has recognized these as reliable medicines to be given for specific ailments.

One of the major problems is providing potable (drinking) water throughout the country. A few years ago less than half of the houses had installed or easy-access piped water. Fewer than that had sewage systems.

Guayaquil's burgeoning population still requires the use of tank trucks to deliver drinking water to some parts of the city. Quito and Guayaquil have purification plants. In smaller cities water purity may vary.

Trash and garbage collection is very good in Quito. In the crowded slum areas of most other cities such collections are lacking. Environmental sanitation is almost nonexistent in the Indian villages. The government sprays and fumigates houses and wearing apparel to eradicate disease-bearing rats and insects.

Above: Fine baskets and mats are made by the Indians.
Below: They also make unusual paper-thin ceramics.
The woman is decorating a pot, using her own hair as a brush.

Chapter 7

THE ARTS AND LEISURE-TIME ACTIVITIES

Handicrafts have been a part of Ecuadorian Indian life for thousands of years. This has been seen in the ancient ceramics that have been unearthed. Other arts practiced by the Indians for centuries include basketry and weaving. They still play an important role in Indian life. These handicrafts provide useful and necessary items. In many cases they also provide additional income.

Stonework and metallurgy were also important crafts. Carved stone statues, beads, and animals were produced in the Costa, especially in the present provinces of Manabí and Esmeraldas. Some are similar to Mayan and Egyptian styles. Metallurgy, especially gold, resulted in attractive ornaments.

RELIGIOUS ART

The conquistadores soon recognized that the Indian was truly an artist. Through the Roman Catholic church, the Indians were encouraged to develop their artistic talents.

Soon after the Spaniards arrived, the Franciscan priests established a school where these talents could be utilized. The Indians were taught European painting, sculpture, wood carving, and metalwork.

A variety of art can be found in Ecuador. Left: An Indian carving of the magi for a Nativity scene. Right: An art exhibit in El Ejido Park in Quito

Soon these works were used to beautify the great European-style churches that were erected. Spanish artists joined the Indians in providing works of art. The result, particularly in Quito, has made the churches of Ecuador some of the most magnificent in all of South America.

Quito's National Museum of Colonial Art exhibits fine works by Miguel Santiago, Bernardo Rodríguez, and Manuel Samaniego. The greatest Indian sculptor was known by his nickname, "Caspicara." The Museum at the Central Bank features displays of archaeology and colonial and modern art.

MODERN ART

Today's painters have produced nationalistic paintings, often large murals. Osvaldo Guayasamín is probably the best known of these nationalistic painters. Guayasamín was born in Quito. His father was Indian and his mother *mestizo.* As a boy of ten he sold his sketches on the streets. By the time he was thirty-six his works were exhibited in the major museums and galleries of the world. His works identify him with the poor and underdeveloped nations.

Less political in theme are the works of Manuel Rendón. His paintings have a luminescent quality.

Other notable artists have studios in Quito. They include Eduardo Kingman, Leonardo Tejada, Osvaldo Viteri, Anibal Villacis, Nelsón Román, and Ramiro Jácome.

Architects, too, have made contributions to the visual arts. In many instances, they have designed new buildings favoring the modern international trend. Concrete, stuccoed brick, and glass have been the materials used on the exteriors. Wood and stone form decorative features.

LITERATURE AND FREEDOM OF EXPRESSION

The Andes Indians did not have a written language. Oral traditions are all that is left today of the folklore of these hardy people. Even the Inca left no written record in Ecuador. What we know of their achievements was recorded by the Spaniards.

The best-known writer of the seventeenth century was Gaspar de Villarroel, an Augustinian priest. His writings covered many topics, including the relationship between church and state.

In the period termed "Enlightenment," the most famous author was Francisco Javier Eugenio de Santa Cruz y Espejo, now a national hero. Toward the end of the eighteenth century, José Joaquín Olmedo wrote strongly for independence.

Freedom of expression was guaranteed by every constitution written since 1830. The press, therefore, has been generally free from government interference.

Juan Montalvo became the voice of the liberal movement. Shortly after the middle of the nineteenth century other forms of literary expression were published. Juan León Mera wrote a novel about the Indians at the time of independence.

Federico González Suárez was the author of four volumes of Ecuadorian history. Other great literary figures included authors Gonzalo Zaldumbide, Luis A. Martínez, Humberto Salvador, Alfonso Cuesta y Cuesta, Jorge Icaza, and playwright Francisco Tobar García. Many of the works of these writers and others such as Pío Jaramillo Alvarado deal with national life.

MUSICAL EXPRESSION

Ritual music with native instruments portrays the folklore of the pre-Columbian Indians. These native instruments are still played by the Sierra Indians. There are flutes made of bamboo or clay and a panpipe fashioned from a series of bamboo reeds.

The Indians in different parts of the country made instruments from materials close at hand: seashells, toucan beaks, gourds filled with seeds, and bulls' horns. Drums were made from hollow logs covered with animal hides.

The music of the Sierra Indians uses a five-tone scale that sounds rather melancholy. *El Sanjuanito,* the national song and dance, is usually sung in the minor key of the Indians.

Left: An Indian flute called a quena
Right: The office of the Casa de la Cultura *in Quito*

The National Symphony Orchestra is based in Quito. It plays many works by Ecuadorian and internationally acclaimed composers. Domenico Brescia, Segundo Luis Moreno, and Luis Salgado have composed symphonies and ballets from folk music.

The National Dance Company performs ballets on occasion. There are often modern presentations as well as those derived from history and folklore.

Several of the country's holidays feature dances in which the performers wear masks symbolizing primitive gods.

African influence in music is found in the Costa. There, the samba and the marimba are enjoyed.

Dramas are frequently presented in two circular Quito theaters. Pedro Traversari has written dramas based on Indian history.

The *Casa de la Cultura* (House of Culture) is a government-sponsored agency that promotes the arts. It began through the efforts of Benjamín Carrión, an author. There are branches in many parts of the country. The main office is in Quito, where

Children playing soccer

there is a permanent exhibit of Ecuadorian arts. The House of Culture also publishes about fifty books a year.

RECREATION

Many Ecuadorians engage in sports during their leisure time. The best athletes participated in the Pan-American games and in the Olympic games in 1984.

Soccer is the national sport. Professional teams compete nationally and internationally. Amateur teams participate in regular leagues. There are also many informal games, particularly on Sunday afternoons.

Basketball is the second most important team sport, followed closely by volleyball.

Pancho González, Ecuador's tennis star for many years, played in Davis Cup matches. In 1984 the world's fifth-ranked tennis player was Andrés Gómez, another Ecuadorian.

Golf, horse racing, table tennis, boating, and mountain climbing are sports enjoyed by only a small segment of society.

Twice-yearly bullfights attract great crowds. They feature

Cockfights are still legal in some areas of Ecuador.

bullfighters of international renown who are touring Latin America.

Cockfights can be seen in pits in small villages as well as in the cities. Usually, only men attend.

Fiestas are exciting community gatherings. No matter what the financial or social status of the people, they participate in fiestas on national or regional holidays.

The foundation of Quito is celebrated for two weeks at the end of November and the beginning of December. On the night of December 5, the people dance and sing the "Serenade of Quito." Throughout the two weeks there are exhibitions as well as folkloric presentations. And there are ten bullfights at the great Bullfight Fair.

A Parade of National Unity with Ecuadorian leaders and members of the foreign diplomatic corps concludes the celebration on December 6.

Weekly markets are held in Latacunga (left) and Riobamba (right).

In the past, fiestas were often sponsored by individuals in honor of baptisms, funerals, or the building of a house. The cost often far exceeded the means of Indian and *mestizo* families.

Market days are still extremely important in the Sierra. Many of the Indians walk great distances to reach the market town, carrying the produce they hope to sell. Market day affords an opportunity to meet other people, to buy and sell, and perhaps to indulge in a piece of roast guinea pig.

Most notable market towns are Otavalo, Ambato, Riobamba, and Latacunga. Each town or city has a specific market day. For a time the Indians can escape the harsh life they endure in the Sierra. Then they trudge home, often carrying some of the handicrafts or vegetables they have been unable to sell. The following week they return to the town for the next market day.

Chapter 8

A DIFFICULT ECONOMY

Ecuador has found it necessary to obtain many millions of dollars in loans from foreign banks and the International Monetary Fund. By 1983 the public external debt was $4.7 billion and the private external debt was $1.5 billion. The government sought to reschedule part of the public debt with two hundred foreign banks. It was not able to meet the payment of $2.4 billion in principal and interest.

Strong measures were necessary to reduce the great budget deficits. Government spending was cut. This resulted in a general strike in March, 1983, after earlier and smaller strikes.

Fortunately, Ecuador did have a favorable balance of trade. Exports were greater in value than imports.

OIL!

Although it is now an oil-producing country, Ecuador is one of the least developed countries in South America. Petroleum had been produced near Salinas in the Santa Elena peninsula since 1911. In 1967 Ecuador became a major petroleum producer after petroleum fields were found in the Oriente.

An oil derrick in a clearing in the jungle

For several years Texaco and Gulf Oil were engaged in the production. Then in 1974 the Ecuadorian State Petroleum Corporation (CEPE) became a partner. At the end of 1976, CEPE bought out Gulf Oil. Together with Texaco it accounted for 97 percent of the country's petroleum production.

A pipeline carries the oil 310 miles (499 kilometers) over the Andes and down to Esmeraldas on the Pacific Ocean.

Great plans were made for this new source of income. The oil was marketed in Asia, Latin America, and the United States. It was hoped the increased revenue would change the social and economic structure. But then inflation, a worldwide recession, and lower petroleum prices altered these plans dramatically.

There has been little exploration for additional oil fields since 1972. By 1983, Ecuador produced about 230,000 barrels of crude oil a day. It accounted for 55 percent of the merchandise exports and 12 percent of the gross domestic product of the country, one third of the central government revenue. About half of the production is used in Ecuador.

Great reserves of natural gas are thought to exist in the Gulf of Guayaquil. Thus far, they have not reached commercial production.

AGRICULTURE

Almost half of the population is employed in agriculture. The most important domestic food crops are rice, corn, barley, and potatoes. El Niño necessitated the importation of rice and other food items in 1983.

There are now a great many small farms and few large farms. Most of the small farms are still operated in primitive ways. Attempts to develop cooperatives so that the owners of small farms could use modern machinery have had little impact.

In 1960, agriculture accounted for 36.8 percent of the gross domestic product. By 1970 it was only 31.1 percent; in 1982, only 11.6 percent. Of course, other products—petroleum and manufactured items, for example—had increased in their shares of the gross domestic product.

The population has increased rapidly, far more so than improvements in agricultural methods to increase production. Greater imports in fats, oils, and wheat have been necessary.

Several crops are grown especially for export. Bananas, cacao, coffee, pineapples, and sugarcane are the most important. But when El Niño devastates these fields, the source of income from exports declines.

Bananas were raised for domestic consumption for many years. By 1948, they were being grown for export also. The main producing areas are along the coast and the lower western slopes of the mountains.

When higher-yielding, disease-resistant varieties of bananas were grown in Central American countries, Ecuador's export market declined. The government recommended that banana growers plant one of the new varieties and cut back on production. Farmers were encouraged to plant other crops or raise livestock on the acreage removed from banana production.

Coffee has been the second or third most valuable crop since its introduction early in the nineteenth century. Over 80 percent of the coffee farms are between 3 and 12 acres (1.2 to 4.9 hectares). More than half of the production is in Manabí Province in the Costa north of Guayaquil.

In good weather the yield is high and surpluses accumulate. In years when there is a drought the yields are low. Production methods have not improved over the years. Few farmers use fertilizer. Irrigation is almost nonexistent. Recently the government has taken measures to regulate coffee production. It must meet quotas set by the International Coffee Agreement and domestic consumption. The government has asked farmers to shift 65,000 acres (26,304 hectares) from coffee into other crops.

Cacao trees produce gourd-shaped pods. The seeds or beans found inside are dried in the sun. Cocoa is made from the beans. The export of processed cocoa has declined, but raw cocoa (cacao beans) exports have increased.

The Indians cultivated cacao long before the Spaniards arrived. The crop was exported by 1655. Ecuador was the largest cacao producer in the world until the end of World War I, when diseases destroyed many of the trees.

By the end of World War II disease-resistant strains were planted. The cacao plantations are located in the Costa. Some of the plantations are large, but many are small or medium sized.

Sugarcane (left) and cocoa (right)

The large plantations use fertilizer and replace older trees. Small plantations use traditional cultivation methods.

Sugar is also a Costa crop. About 2.5 million tons (2.3 metric tonnes) of cane are produced in a normal year. The plantations are large and mostly owned by the sugar mills.

Farmers in the Sierra grow small quantities of cane. It is made into raw brown-sugar cakes. Molasses is a sugarcane by-product. Some molasses is exported, while part is used to manufacture alcohol or in livestock feed.

Rice is raised in the floodplain of the Costa. There are two annual crops. The large winter crop is harvested from May through June. A smaller crop, planted in summer, is harvested in September and October.

The greatest amount of cropland is planted in corn, or maize. Most is grown in the Sierra, where eight to ten months are required for crop maturity. Corn can be grown from sea level to 9,500 feet (2,896 meters). The use of more fertilizer and improved varieties has increased production. Much of the corn is used for animal feed, especially for poultry. About half is grown for human consumption.

The Sierra is well suited to potato crops. The high, cool regions have increased yield. Sierra farmers keep their crop in the ground until sold. Many of the potatoes rot. More aboveground storage facilities would increase the yield.

Barley was introduced by the Spaniards. It thrives high in the Sierra. Improved strains have increased yield. It is raised as a food grain and for the brewing industry.

For many years wheat growing was of little importance. The government hopes to make the country self-sufficient in wheat production. Most of the grain is made into flour for white bread. The Sierra is best suited for growing wheat.

Ecuador is not self-sufficient in raising cotton as yet. Efforts are being made to improve the quality. Grown in the Costa, it is a low-income crop. Through trade regulations, improved strains, and better marketing, the government hopes to decrease the annual imports of cotton for use in textile mills.

The biggest source of vegetable oil has been from the African palm, first planted commercially in 1959. Prior to that, royal palms growing wild in the tropical rain forests were the chief source of vegetable oil. The yield from the African palm is greater than from the royal palm. The trees mature faster. However, the oil content in the royal palm nuts is higher.

Ecuador is the world's major castor bean producer and exporter. Castor beans are usually planted in the same fields as peanuts, corn, and cotton. New high-yielding varieties can produce three or four times as much oil per acre of beans. Exporting the oil is more profitable than exporting the beans. A castor-seed-oil-crushing plant was opened in 1970.

A nontoxic insecticide is produced from pyrethrum, a species of chrysanthemum. The flowers are grown on farms high in the Sierra. Indian women are generally hired to pick the flowers. Processing plants turn the flowers into powder. Kenya and Tanzania compete with Ecuador in production. The yield is higher and the production costs lower in those African countries.

Tea was a new crop introduced in 1965. The first exports were made in 1968. Year-round production can be managed on the eastern slopes of the Andes. The center of tea production is near Puyo at an altitude of 3,000 feet (914 meters). Rainfall averages between 90 and 110 inches (229 and 279 centimeters) annually. Even on a small farm of 12 acres (4.8 hectares) a farmer can make a living growing tea.

ANIMAL HUSBANDRY

One fourth of the total agricultural production is in livestock. There is little left to export. Most is for domestic consumption.

Guinea pigs are raised inside or on the outdoor porch or patio of rural homes. Sometimes weaving looms stand nearby. The guinea pigs are not pets. They are intended for family consumption or for selling at the local market.

Many peasant women care for a few chickens. The eggs and chickens are usually sold in the market to provide extra income for the family. Chicken costs as much per pound as beef.

Cattle serve as work animals as well as milk and beef producers. Even with a million beef and almost a million dairy cattle, the supply is often insufficient for domestic demands. Only about half of the dairy cattle actually produce milk. Dairy cattle are raised in the Sierra.

Only about half of the milk is pasteurized. Pasteurized milk is available in all of the cities, but butter is seldom available outside Quito and Guayaquil. Raw milk is sold in the villages and small towns. Milk supplies only a very small portion of the calories consumed daily by children and adults.

To encourage construction of pasteurizing plants, Quito banned the sale of raw milk. There are several cheese factories located in the highlands.

Since beef is not aged, it is usually tough. The price is high, above the means of most people.

Few farmers have as many as fifty head of beef cattle. Fewer than two hundred ranches have herds of five hundred or more. Most beef cattle are raised in the Costa. More recently, small herds have been introduced in the Oriente. It is hoped that larger herds will be raised there.

Many problems face livestock owners. Often the quality of the pasturage decreases. The Livestock Association of the Sierra imports seed to improve pastures. It is made available without charge to farmers. But many farmers do not avail themselves of this offer.

There are few veterinarians in the country to treat ailing animals. Many cattle have hoof-and-mouth disease, ticks, or internal parasites. Attempts to improve the breeding stock have been insignificant.

Sheep can be found at altitudes above 9,000 feet (2,900 meters). A few can also be found in the Costa and the Oriente. The Spanish conquistadores introduced sheep to Ecuador.

Many Indians and *mestizos* in the Sierra raise a few sheep. If they do not know how to shear the sheep to obtain wool, they may sell the animals for a very small sum.

Pigs and fish for sale at local markets

About half of the sheep are raised on *haciendas.* The government has imported good breeding rams and sold them to farmers at low cost. The intent is to improve the quality of the wool.

Small farmers often raise a few hogs to provide a cash income.

FISHING

The fishing industry usually increases its production annually. Tuna, the skipjack bonita variety, is caught within 20 miles (34 kilometers) offshore. Most of the fishing vessels are small and lack refrigeration. New 90-foot-long (27-meter) refrigerated ships are replacing some of the smaller ships.

Shrimp is the second most important catch. Most come from the Gulf of Guayaquil. El Niño actually helped the shrimp catch.

Herring, including sardines and anchovies, are caught to make fish meal for poultry feed.

There are many saltwater varieties of fish that increase the food supply for the Costa. There are at least 273 species of freshwater fish in Ecuador. Trout hatcheries have been established so that lakes and rivers in the Sierra can be stocked.

Ecuador claims territorial rights 200 miles (322 kilometers) out into the Pacific. This has led to some misunderstanding with United States fishermen, who have been fined when they fished in these waters. American vessels have caught great quantities of tuna in Ecuadorian-claimed territory.

FORESTRY

More than 2,200 species of trees grow in Ecuador. Most of the forested land belongs to the government.

Unfortunately, Sierra forests have been cut down to provide farm and grazing land. The wood was used as fuel and in construction.

In 1860 eucalyptus trees were brought from Australia. They grow well in Ecuador's Sierra. They are used for lumber and fuel. Where there are large plantings, they prevent soil erosion.

The Costa supplies the country with both hardwood and softwood. Balsa (a very light wood), kapok for stuffings, and rubber in small quantities contribute to the economy.

The toquilla palm tree supplies fiber from which the women weave the famed panama hats—made in Ecuador, not Panama!

MINERALS AND MINING

Many regions in which valuable minerals could be mined are difficult to reach. Legally, all minerals belong to the state. Private companies can obtain permission to mine them.

Limestone, copper, and gold are the three most valuable

Left: After a weaver has made a panama hat, it is sold to someone who finishes it. Right: Panning for gold

minerals. Usually silver is also found where there is gold. Sulfur, zinc, cadmium, and lead are also mined.

INDUSTRIALIZATION

Manufacturing has increased rapidly in the past decade. Canned foods, beverages, and textiles have led the list. Many plants are small, employing no more than five persons.

Guayaquil is the chief industrial city, with breweries, food processing plants, tanneries, sawmills, iron foundries, and sugar mills. Flour mills process imported wheat into white flour.

Quito has textile mills, flour mills, a tannery, and other manufacturing plants that provide employment.

The opportunity for employment in the industrial sector draws thousands to the cities from rural areas annually.

Chapter 9

ECUADOR AND THE WORLD

EXPORTS AND IMPORTS

In normal years, agricultural crops are not affected by very heavy rains and flooding. Then Ecuador is the world's largest exporter of bananas. More than 50 percent of the total exports are bananas.

Some of the banana exporting is done by foreign fruit companies. Other companies are Ecuadorian owned. For many years the entire stalk, with hundreds of bananas in "hands," was cut green and transported in the refrigerated holds of ships.

Now, sometimes the "hands" are removed from the stalks, packed in boxes, and then shipped in the refrigerated holds.

Coffee has been the country's second most important export. Prices paid for Ecuadorian coffee are often lower than those paid to other countries. Coffee plantation owners have not adopted modern techniques. The beans are of uneven quality.

Cacao, the source of chocolate, is usually the third most important export. Sugar had played a major role in exports. However, the per capita consumption of sugar has dropped as more artificial sweeteners are used.

"Hands" of bananas being loaded on a ship for export. Bananas that are considered below quality standards are dumped on the quay.

Fish products have increased in sales abroad. Canned tuna, shrimp, frozen fish, and lobster are exported. Much of the shrimp is cleaned and deveined. Low wages enable the industry to compete with other shrimp-exporting countries.

In 1983 the United States lifted its ban on the importation of Ecuadorian tuna.

The sale of petroleum has enabled the country to reach a favorable balance of payments in some years. However, the price of petroleum products has decreased since 1983. There has been a decrease in the balance of payments in both crude and refined petroleum products.

For many years the United States has been Ecuador's chief trading partner. About one third of the country's exports are sent to the United States. Ecuador's imports are mainly from the United States, Japan, and West Germany.

The 1980-84 National Development Plan had to trim its public-sector spending because of budget deficits. However, the demand for imports of manufactured products continued.

Machines of all types are principal imports. Farm, communication, and transportation equipment are in great demand. Increased labor costs, inflation, high interest rates for loans abroad, and a shortage of trained managers have hampered industrial development. Until Ecuador can increase its industrial output, it will continue to import much of its consumer and industrial needs.

TRANSPORTATION

For thousands of years all travel was on foot. The Indians did not have horses or mules. They walked, even as they do today.

Many of Ecuador's roads follow Indian trails. The oldest and most heavily traveled road is the Pan-American Highway. It follows the Inca Imperial Highway through the Sierra. For 728 miles (1,172 kilometers) it connects towns from Tulcán, on the border with Colombia, to Macará on Peru's border.

Similarly, a highway connects Guayaquil and Esmeraldas. Four highways were constructed to connect the Pan-American Highway with the Costa. More and more goods are shipped by truck. New trading communities have grown up along these roads.

New roads were necessary to connect the Sierra with the Oriente and the oil fields. Communities along these roads increased in size and importance. New agricultural centers were developed. Resettlement centers were established.

Road maintenance is sometimes poor. Mudslides and washouts may make roads impassable.

Most trucks are driver owned. They seldom follow a schedule. Shipping rates may vary. There are many small trucking

A passenger bus in Quito

companies. Some driver-owners and companies belong to cooperatives. The cooperatives develop set rates and establish schedules.

Intercity buses are plentiful. Most of the bus drivers and owners belong to a cooperative. They maintain fairly regular schedules. Bus and truck traffic between Quito and Guayaquil is the heaviest in the country.

Intercity railroad service is limited. The Quito-Guayaquil Railroad was completed in 1908. Where previously twelve days were required to make the trip, the railroad took only twelve hours. The route was 281 miles (452 kilometers) long. Travel was disrupted when landslides destroyed the tracks in 1983 during the El Niño season.

On the Quito-Guayaquil line an auto-ferro (one-car diesel train) is a favorite with tourists. Many people stop in Riobamba on market day. There are several other short lines that operate between two cities. All lines are single track.

The State Railways Company owns about sixty locomotives, five hundred freight cars, and forty passenger cars.

A railroad station near Chimborazo in the Sierra

The railroads went into disrepair when the government stressed highway construction. President Guillermo Rodríguez Lara began a three-year plan of reconstruction in 1972.

Airplanes now link many of Ecuador's cities. There are many daily flights between Guayaquil and Quito, as well as to Cuenca, Esmeraldas, Manta, Machala, Portoviejo, Tulcán, and Loja. There are also flights to the Oriente, which land at Coca and Lago Agrio. Special flights to other locales can also be arranged.

There are also several flights each week to Baltra, an island in the Galápagos Islands. Ships for the Galápagos sail from Guayaquil. TAME airlines uses Guayaquil's international airport for departures and arrivals.

Tourism is still undeveloped, but there is now a National Tourism Office. It promotes travel to Ecuador, the cities, the beautiful beaches, the Andes, the Oriente, and the Galápagos. Ecuadorian Airlines features special tours, as do other airlines.

The waterways of the Guayas Basin are important routes for domestic commerce. Coastal shipping is very well developed, too. Five miles (7 kilometers) up the Guayas River is the busy new port of Guayaquil. Foreign ships tie up at its five general docks:

three container-loading docks, one for specialized cargo, and one for small vessels. Twenty-four large warehouses have been constructed. In 1977 enlargement of the port facilities began. The work was completed in April, 1981. It is now a major seaport on international maritime routes.

About 95 percent of the value of all exports and imports are moved by sea. Although Guayaquil's harbor handles most of the foreign shipping, Manta exports frozen fish, coffee, and castor beans. More than half of the bananas are shipped from Puerto Bolívar. Esmeraldas handles petroleum and bananas. There are other ports along the Pacific Ocean as well.

COMMUNICATION

The government reports a literacy rate of 85 percent. Whether or not that is higher than the actual percentage, there is a great need for mass communcation.

Many areas of the country are isolated. News and entertainment are supplied to them by radio. There are over 600,000 radio sets in use, with an average daily listening audience of over 7,000,000.

Two municipally owned stations and the government's Radio Nacional are the only stations not privately operated. More than 350 stations, 35 of them FM, are licensed by the government but are free to do their own programming. Only some stations in Quito and Guayaquil are high powered.

Television, too, is licensed by the government but is independent and privately owned. There are ten color TV stations in five cities. Several stations can reach a nationwide audience through repeater stations. The potential audience is over three million. There are about 600,000 sets in use.

Telephones and telecommunications link the major cities with automatic dialing. There are more than 100,000 telephones in use, primarily in the large cities. Domestic telegrams can also be sent.

International calls can be made via satellite. A ground station operates near Quito.

Thirty-two daily newspapers are published in twelve cities. Weekly newspapers are published in many smaller towns. Quito's *El Comercio* has a circulation of over 100,000. *El Universo*, published in Guayaquil, has a circulation of over 120,000. Total newspaper readership is over half a million, with a daily circulation of more than 410,000.

Thirty magazines are published in the country. The most popular are *Vistazo* (general interest), *Estadio* (sports), and a women's magazine, *Hogar.* American magazines and newspapers are flown in and are available in the shops in the major hotels. French, German, and British magazines also can be purchased.

Most of the motion pictures shown in the 235 theaters are American. There is no feature film industry in Ecuador. Films are popular, however. Those from the United States generally have Spanish subtitles or dialogue dubbed in Spanish. Annual attendance at the movies is estimated at almost five million.

Ecuador enjoys freedom of speech and the press. There is no censorship of its radio broadcasts. This freedom of expression, guaranteed by all constitutions since 1830, has played an important role in the political and cultural life of the people.

A ROLE IN THE WORLD

Ecuador's relations with the United States have been close. Economic development has been assisted directly through the U.S.

Agency for International Development (AID). The Peace Corps also has had a large program in the country.

The United States maintains a major exchange program established in 1956. In 1982 four American university lecturers taught for short terms in Ecuadorian institutions. Twenty Ecuadorian students received grants to study in the United States and at least four U.S. graduate students did research in Ecuador.

The United States Information Service maintains a library to provide officials and professionals with relevant materials.

The two countries also have been linked through participation in the Organization of American States, the United Nations, and various commissions within the United Nations.

The United Nations Economic Commission on Latin America met in Quito in 1973. Colombia, Venezuela, Peru, Bolivia, and Ecuador have formed the Andean Pact to coordinate efforts on behalf of future development.

Many other countries have active cultural and educational exchange programs with Ecuador. The most active programs are carried on by Brazil, Cuba, France, Great Britain, Israel, Japan, The Netherlands, Spain, the United States, USSR, and West Germany. Many countries offer scholarships for study abroad.

Diplomatic relations are maintained with all of the Western European countries and with many countries in the Middle East, Asia, and the Western Hemisphere. Forty-five countries maintain embassies in Quito. Some countries also maintain consular offices in Guayaquil.

Ecuador has been a member of the Latin American Free Trade Association (LAFTA) and the Andean Common Market. LAFTA was organized to achieve full free trade by 1980 through annual tariff reductions.

Ecuador is also a member of the Latin American Economic System, Latin American Energy Association, and two economic integration associations—Latin American Integration Association and the Andean Pact.

Although it is one of the smaller petroleum exporting countries, it belongs to the Organization of Petroleum Exporting Countries (OPEC).

Colombia and Ecuador have joined in a border tariff accord. It enables all residents in the provinces along the joint border to trade without customs duties or other restrictions. There have been some problems with smuggling, however.

ECUADOR'S FUTURE

There are many obstacles to Ecuador's progress. Its geographical features, with the towering volcanic Andes, the steamy jungle and rain forest, and the arid southern Costa, present problems that so far defy solutions. Only 17 percent of the land is arable.

The country holds great potential in its natural and human resources. With creativity and innate ability, the citizenry could achieve much through education and new opportunities for service and work.

The low productivity per worker, low per capita income, and general social conditions hinder progress.

Even the weather at times seems to conspire against the country.

Instability in government for many years prevented foreign investment that would have helped the economy.

The integration of the Indian and the *mestizo* into society and the opening of job opportunities regardless of social status are

In the background of the city of Riobamba is Sangay Volcano (above). Volcanoes, jungles, rain forests, and other geographic features present problems to Ecuador's progress, but the country has placed its hope in its citizens, such as the young mestizo *(left) and the school children (right) from Guano.*

Left: Homes on the waterfront in Guayaquil Right: Barley growing in the Sierra

keys to future development. This will require expanded education and job training opportunities.

Population growth must be slowed, however, if employment rates are to rise. With great migration from the Sierra to the cities, the many unskilled workers cannot be absorbed into the economy.

With a primarily agrarian economy, Ecuador is at the mercy of price fluctuations for its products. Through the Andean Pact, the five signatory countries hope to address this problem.

To increase agricultural productivity, measures must be taken to reduce soil erosion. Better methods of farming, use of farm machinery, applications of fertilizer, improvement in breeding stock, and better storage facilities are necessary.

The gap between the upper and lower classes in society is very

An Otavalo Indian family

pronounced. A high degree of illiteracy prevails. The middle class is still relatively small. More schools and trained teachers are needed.

Malnutrition must be combated. Health and sanitation services must be expanded.

The people have shown remarkable resilience. They survived invasions by the Inca and then by the Spaniards. The Indians have maintained much of their own culture.

The tremendous national debt drains much of the profit from exports. The budget deficit must be addressed also.

Ecuador has the potential to leave the ranks of the underdeveloped countries through restraints in government spending and the utilization of its human and natural resources.

MAP KEY

Place	Grid
Aguarico (river)	B2
Alausí	B2
Alfaro	B2
Ambato	B2
Arenillas	B1
Azogues	B2
B. Isabel	g5
B. de Ancón de Sardinas	A2
B. de Bamcos	g5
B. de Santa Elena	B1
Babahoyo	B2
Baeza	B2
Bahía de Caráquez	B1
Balzar	B2
Baños	B2
C. Berkeley	g5
C. San Mateo	B1
Cabo Pasado (cape)	B1
Cabo de San Francisco (cape)	A1
Calceta	B1
Cañar	B2
Cariamanga	B2
Catacocha	B2
Catamayo	B2
Cayambe (mountain)	A2
Cayambe	A2
Celica	B1
Chimborazo (mountain)	B2
Chone	B1
Cotopaxi (mountain)	B2
Cuenca	B2
Curaray (river)	B2
Daule	A2
Daule	B2
El Corazón	B2
El Progreso	g6
Esmeraldas	A2
Fierro Urco (mountain)	B2
Francisco de Orellano	B2
Golfo de Guayaquil	B1
Gualaceo	B2
Gualaquiza	B2
Guaranda	B2
Guayaquil	B2
I. Baltra	g5
I. Darwin	f5
I. Española (Hood)	g6
I. Fernandina (Narborough)	g5
I. Genovesa	f6
I. Marchena	f5
I. Pinta	f5
I. Pinzón	g5
I. San Crístóbal (Chatham)	g6
I. San Salvador (James)	g5
I. Sta. Cruz (Indefatigable)	g6
I. Sta. Fé	g5
I. Sta. María	g5
I. Wolf	f5
Ibarra	A2
Isla Isabela (Albemarle I.)	g6
Isla Puná	B1
Jipijapa	B1
La Puntilla	B1
Latacunga	B2
Loja	B2
Macará	B2
Macas	B2
Machachi	B2
Machala	B2
Manta	B1
Marro	B1
Mira (river)	B2
Montecristi	B1
Napo (river)	B2
Otavalo	A2
Palmira	B2
Pasaje Girón	B2
Pastaza (river)	B2
Píllaro	B2
Portoviejo	B1
Pta. Albemarle	f5
Pta. Essex	g5
Puebloviejo	B2
Puerto Bolívar	B2
Pujili	B2
Puyo	B2
Quito	B2
Riobamba	B2
Rocafuerte	B1
S. Miguel (river)	A2
Salcedo	B2
Salinas	B1
San Gabriel	A2
San Lorenzo	A2
Santa Ana	B1
Santa Elena	B1
Santa Rosa	B2
Santo Domingo de los Colorados	B2
Saraguro	B2
Sigsig	B2
Tena	B2
Tulcán	A2
Valladolid	B2
Villamil	g5
Vinces	B2
Vol. Sangay	B2
Volcán Wolf	f5
Yaguachi	B2
Yaupi	B2
Zamara (river)	B2
Zamora	B2
Zapotillo	B1
Zaruma	B2

Abbreviations used:

B.—bay
C.—cape
I.—island
Pta.—point
Vol.—volcano

© Copyright by Rand McNally & Co. R.L. 85-S-104

MINI-FACTS AT A GLANCE

GENERAL INFORMATION

Official Name: *República del Ecuador* (Republic of Ecuador)

Capital: Quito

Official Language: Spanish; Indian dialects (especially Quechua) are also spoken.

Government: Ecuador is a democratic republic. It has had more than fifteen constitutions since 1822, when it seceded from Spain. The constitution of 1979 established a formal separation of powers with a president elected by popular, direct, and secret voting for a four-year term. Members of the Chamber of Deputies are elected for two-year terms. Two senators are elected from each of the twenty provinces for four-year terms. In addition, fifteen senators are chosen at large by various interest groups, such as the armed forces, the universities, agricultural interests on the coast, etc. The judiciary, as in most countries that have not been part of the Anglo-American tradition of common law, plays only a marginal political role. There are many political parties, but none has been dominant in recent years.

Religion: The overwhelming majority of the people are Catholic. Less than 1 percent are Protestant. Religious freedom is guaranteed.

Flag: The upper half is yellow. The lower half has two horizontal bars, blue above red. The colors are those of the Republic of Greater Colombia, of which Ecuador was a part until 1830.

Coat of Arms: The national coat of arms is at the center of the flag. Adopted in 1822, it shows a condor, Chimborazo Mountain, and the first steamboat built in Ecuador.

National Anthem: *"Himno Nacional del Ecuador"* ("National Anthem of Ecuador")

Money: Basic unit—sucre. One hundred centavos equal one sucre. In September of 1987, one U.S. dollar was approximately equal to 196.5 sucres.

Weights and Measures: Ecuador uses the metric system.

Population: Estimated 1987 population—9,922,514; 35 percent rural, 65 percent urban; density, 94.95 persons per sq. mi. (36.7 persons per km^2); 1982 census—8,060,712. Population increases from 1977 to 1986 are estimated at 2.9 percent per year. Using this percentage increase, the 1990 population will total approximately 10,811,059.

Cities:

	1982 Census	Mid-1986 Estimate
Guayaquil	1,199,344	1,509,108
Quito	866,472	1,093,278
Cuenca	152,406	193,012
Machala	105,521	137,321
Portoviejo	102,628	134,393

GEOGRAPHY

Highest Point: Chimborazo Mountain, 20,561 ft. (6,267 m)

Lowest Point: Sea level

Rivers: The Guayas is part of the largest river system on the Pacific coast of South America. It is formed by the juncture of the Daule and the Babahoyo rivers and is navigable for much of its course. Other rivers that flow toward the ocean are the Santiago and the Cayapas and their tributaries: the Esmeraldas, the Jubones, and the Santa Rosa. The Napa River flows eastward until it joins the Amazon River.

Mountains: The Andes highlands, often called the Sierra, lies between the coastal and eastern lowlands. It makes up about one fourth of Ecuador. Two parallel ridges of the Andes Mountains extend the length of the country from north to south. Several of the mountains—Sangay, Tunguragua, and Cotopaxi—are active volcanoes.

Climate: Ecuador's seasons are often the opposite of those in the Northern Hemisphere. The climate varies according to the altitude. The lowlands are hot and humid. The Peru Current cools the coastal lowlands slightly. The temperature in the lowlands averages about 75° F. (24° C). The Galápagos Islands (a group of islands off the coast that belong to Ecuador) have a tropical climate cooled by the Peru Current.

The plateaus in the Andes highlands have a springlike climate all year, with an average temperature of 57° F. (14° C). The climate is colder at higher altitudes. Snow covers the Andes upward from about 16,000 ft. (4,879 m).

Rain falls from January to May and, in the northwest, all year round.

Greatest Distances: North to south—450 mi. (724 km)
East to west—395 mi. (636 km)
Coastline—1,278 mi. (2,057 km), including the Galápagos

Area: 109,484 sq. mi. (283,561 km²)

NATURE

Trees: The wet lowlands are covered with a tropical rain forest containing dense trees, climbing vines, and epiphytes, which derive nutrients from the air and rain. In the Guayas Valley the forest is largely made up of balsa; in the eastern forest cinchona trees (a source of quinine) are plentiful. The cinchona is the national tree. Flowering trees—acacias, flamboyant, and magnolia—are common.

In the coastal region between Esmeraldas and the Gulf of Guayaquil, the forest gives way to palms and carludovica, which is used for panama hats.

Fish: The fish population is similar to that of the Amazon River. In fresh waters, catfish, arapaima, and rainbow trout are found. In coastal waters, migratory skipjack tuna (from January to April) are of great importance to the fishing industry. Other fish include mackerel, snapper, haddock, sardines, thread herring, swordfish, and squid. Sea bass are also an important part of Ecuador's lucrative fishing industry.

Animals: In the forests there are monkeys of all sizes, from tiny titi to howler monkeys. In the jungle regions are tapirs, anteaters, sloths, armadillos, and lizards. Dangerous snakes, including bushmasters, fer-de-lance, and anacondas, are prevalent.

Smaller animals include porcupines, opossums, rabbits, and squirrels. Jaguars, pumas, and small tigrillos inhabit the highlands. Llamas are found mainly in Riobamba Province. Carnivorous animals include foxes, coatimundis, giant otters, raccoons, skunks, and weasels.

On the Galápagos Islands can be found giant tortoises, land and marine iguanas, huge sea turtles, sea lions, and fur seals.

Birds: Over 1,500 species have been identified. Giant condors, eagles, hawks, hummingbirds, parrots, macaws, toucans, herons, flamingos, and jacamars are among them. The Galápagos penguins and flightless cormorants are unique to these islands.

Many North American birds migrate to Ecuador for the winter. These include the Virginia rail, the kingbird, the barn swallow, and the scarlet tanager.

EVERYDAY LIFE

Food: The Ecuadorian diet is based on corn, beans, and potatoes. Most of the food for the people in the cities is grown on *haciendas* in the Andes highlands. Grains and vegetables are the main crops. Farmers raise cattle for meat and dairy products. Fish is important to the diet—and plentiful.

In the Sierra the Indian diet usually consists of one-dish meals, or a fried potato cake containing cheese and topped with an egg, called *llapingacho. Humitas,* sweet corn cooked in the husk, is like a tamale. Plátano, a large, bananalike fruit, is fried, baked, toasted, or prepared as a cake. *Empanadas* are wheat pastries filled with meat and cheese. Fish soup is often made with green peas, toasted ground peanuts, cheese, and potatoes.

Housing: Half of Ecuador's housing consists of *casas* (houses) or *villas* (houses with gardens). They are constructed of brick, stone, concrete, or wood. The other half are made of adobe, cane, reed, or other less permanent materials. In the Indian villages most houses are one-room mud huts with thatch roofs. There is a great need for more houses to serve the rapidly increasing population.

Holidays:

January 1, New Year's Day
May 1, Labor Day
May 24, Battle of Pichincha
August 10, National Independence Day
October 12, Columbus Day
November 2, All Souls' Day
December 24, Christmas Day

July 24, Bolívar's Birthday, is legally recognized but rarely observed.

Local holidays include:

August 10, Independence of Quito
October 9, Guayaquil Independence
November 3, Independence of Cuenca
December 6, Founding of Quito

A variety of saints' days and other religious or semireligious holidays are celebrated locally. Carnival is celebrated in the larger urban centers just before Ash Wednesday.

Culture: Though there is a high rate of illiteracy in Ecuador (almost 35 percent) and a poor economy, the level of culture is quite high. Painters tend to use Indian themes, and mural painting on nationalistic and historic subjects is also typical. Osvaldo Guayasamín is perhaps the best-known muralist. His works can be seen in the major museums and galleries of the world. There is a flourishing art colony in Quito.

Literature also often focuses on Indian themes. The poem *Boletín y elegía de las mitas (Record and Elegy on Indian Forced Labor)* by the late Cuencan poet, César Dávila Andrade, is a leading example.

Music seems to be everywhere and is characterized by its sadness. The *yarabi,* among the most popular folk songs, tell of the solitude of the Andes and the oppression of the Indians.

The House of Ecuadorian Culture was established in 1944 to promote and preserve all aspects of the national culture. The National Library, National History Archives, Museum of Colonial Art, and the Pedro Traversari Musical Instrument Museum are some of its subdivisions.

Sports and Recreation: Sports are a leisure-time activity in Ecuador. Athletes participate in the Pan-American games and in the Olympics. Soccer is the national sport, and basketball and volleyball are also popular. Pancho González and Andrés Gómez were world-ranked tennis players. Bullfights and cockfights attract large crowds. Fiestas and market days attract people from all walks of life.

Communication: There are seventeen daily newspapers in Ecuador. *El Universo,* the largest, is published in Guayaquil. There are ten television stations, all privately owned. The country also has about three hundred radio stations. The telephone service is operated by the government; there are about three phones for every two hundred persons.

Transportation: Ecuador's road system is only partially developed because of the nation's rough topography and lack of economic development. Especially in the southern Sierra and the eastern regions, the farmer who wishes to take his products to market must frequently use horses or mules.

There are about 13,000 miles (20,921 kilometers) of roads, of which about 1,800 miles (2,986 kilometers) are paved. The Pan-American Highway crosses the country from north to south.

Railroads total about 700 miles (1,127 kilometers), but service is poor and they are used more for freight than for passengers. Most of the major cities have airports, and international flights stop at Quito and Guayaquil.

Schools: Although the government requires all children between six and fourteen years of age to attend school, many rural children in fact do not attend school at all. Most schools are operated by the national government. The nation has five public universities, two private universities, and two technical schools. Many affluent Ecuadorians send their children abroad for their higher education.

Health: There are few hospitals or clinics in rural areas, and diseases such as tuberculosis and dysentery are common. Many of the poor also suffer from malnutrition. The government is working to improve the nation's health.

All public and private employees are affiliated with the National Social Security Institute, which provides medical and hospital insurance coverage, retirement pensions, and aid to widows and orphans.

Principal Products:
Agriculture: Bananas, barley, cacao, cattle, coffee, corn, cotton, pyrethrum, rice, sugar, vegetables, and wheat
Forestry: Balsa wood, tagua nuts
Manufacturing: Building materials, crude steel, cement, chemicals, petroleum products, drugs, flour, processed foods, hats, leather, textiles
Mining: Copper, gold, petroleum, sulfur

IMPORTANT DATES

c.9000 B.C.—Civilization exists high in the Andes near Quito

c.1000 B.C. —Farmers living in Monjashuaico Province of Azuay

c.A.D. 1200—Aymara and Quechua nations found a state in Cuzco, Peru

c.1455-1460—Inca invade land to the north of Peru

early 1500s—Spaniards in Panama hear tales of a rich kingdom in the south

1533—Francisco Pizarro and his men execute Atahualpa, the Inca king, in northern Peru

1534—Spanish town of San Francisco de Quito founded by Sebastián de Benalcázar on December 6

1541—Gonzalo Pizarro, Francisco Pizarro's brother, sets out from Quito to find gold

1542—Spanish crown establishes the New Laws, which are less severe on the Indians of Ecuador

1548—Order is restored in Quito

1563—*Audiencia* of Quito granted the right to deal directly with the Council of the Indies

1739—*Audiencia* of Quito transferred from the viceroyalty of Lima to the viceroyalty of New Granada

1767—Jesuits expelled from Ecuador

1809—Juan Pío Montúfar leads *criollo* patriots in cry for independence

1811—Independence is declared; state of Quito is established

1812—Constitution drafted and approved

1820—Ecuador, Colombia, and Venezuela unite under Simón Bolívar to fight for independence; Guayaquil sets up government council, declaring independence from the *Audiencia*

1822—Ecuador and Guayaquil join the Federation of Gran Colombia; Bolívar leads Gran Colombia in war for liberation of Peru; independence forces defeat Spaniards in Battle of Pichincha

1825—War for liberation of Peru ends

1828—Border dispute fought between Peru and Gran Colombia

1829—General Juan José Flores and Ecuadorians defeat Peruvians in Battle of Tarqui

1830—Gran Columbia dissolved; Colombia, Venezuela, and Ecuador become separate republics; Ecuador drafts constitution

1843—Flores-controlled congress prepares a new constitution known as the Charter of Slavery

1845—Revolution ends Flores's rule; a government is set up in Guayaquil

1852—Slavery abolished

1860—Gabriel García Moreno becomes dictator; eucalyptus trees introduced from Australia

1875—García Moreno assassinated

1895—General Eloy Alfaro becomes president; civil war begins

1908—Quito-Guayaquil railroad completed

1912—Alfaro murdered in Quito

1925—Young military officers revolt, seize power, and attempt to reform political and economic systems

1935—Colombia cedes to Peru land claimed by Ecuador

1941—Peru invades an area in the Oriente

1942—After defeat by a Peruvian invading force, Ecuador accepts, then later rejects, terms of Rio Protocol awarding large eastern territory to Peru

1948—Election of Galo Plaza Lasso

1964—Agrarian Reform Law enacted

1965—Tea production introduced

1967—Ecuador becomes major petroleum producer

1970—President José María Velasco Ibarra dissolves the legislature; capturing animals on the endangered species list is banned

1979—Jaime Roldós Aguilera becomes president in free elections

1981—Vice-president Osvaldo Hurtado becomes president on death of Roldós; new port of Guayaquil completed

1982-83—Heavy rains from El Niño cause severe damage

1983—Government spending cuts cause general strike

1984—León Febres Cordero becomes president; Ecuador attends conference in Mexico City on population growth and its problems

1986—Ecuador becomes first oil-exporting country to receive U.S. aid because of falling oil prices

1987—Devastating earthquakes damage oil pipeline halting oil production and exports and causing suspension of interest payments on foreign debt; workers stage general strike to protest austerity measures imposed by government to recover financial losses following the earthquakes

1988—Rodrigo Borja Cevallos of the Democratic Left Party is elected president

IMPORTANT PEOPLE

Eloy Alfaro (1864-1912), general and politician, president from 1897 to 1901 and 1906 to 1911

Atahualpa (c.1502-1533), last of the Inca kings

Sebastián de Benalcázar (1495-1551), Spanish conquistador under Pizarro's command who founded Quito, December 6, 1534

Simón Bolívar (1783-1830), Venezuelan soldier, statesman, and revolutionary leader known as the Liberator of South America

Atauqui Duchicela Shyri XIII, king of Shyri nation

Hualcopo Duchicela Shyri XIV, king of Shyri nation

Francisco Javier Eugenio de Santa Cruz y Espejo (1747-1796), doctor, writer, and revolutionary leader

Juan José Flores (1800-1864), general, first president of Ecuador

Guillermo Franco, tried to put Guayaquil and southern Ecuador under Peruvian rule

Huayna-Capac (d.1535), son of Inca king Tupac-Yupanqui

Juan León Mera (1832-1894), novelist

Juan Montalvo (1832-1889), writer and liberal leader

Juan Pío Montúfar, patriot

Vasco Núñez de Balboa (1475-1519), Spanish explorer, discovered Pacific Ocean

Francisco de Orellana (c.1490-c.1546), Spanish soldier and explorer, discovered the Amazon River

José Joaquín Olmedo (1782-1847), politician and poet

Francisco Pizarro (c.1475-1541), Spanish conqueror of Inca Empire

Gonzalo Pizarro (1502?-1548), governor of Quito, brother of Francisco Pizarro

Lasso Galo Plaza (d.1987), president of Ecuador from 1948 to 1952; secretary general of Organization of American States from 1968 to 1975

Rumiñahui, Inca general

José de San Martín (1778-1850), soldier and statesman

Shyri, king of Caras nation living along the coast in pre-Inca times

Antonio José de Sucre (1795-1830), Bolívar's field marshal

Tupac-Yupanqui (d.1493), Inca king from 1471 to 1493

INDEX

Page numbers that appear in boldface type indicate illustrations

About the Author

Emilie Utteg Lepthien earned BS and MA degrees and a Certificate in School Administration from Northwestern University. She taught third grade, upper-grade science and social studies, and was principal of Wicker Park School in Chicago.

Mrs. Lepthien has written and narrated science and social studies scripts for WBEZ of the Chicago Board of Education. She has been a co-author of primary social studies books for Rand McNally and Company and has served as educational consultant for Encyclopaedia Britannica Films. She is the author of *Penguins, Cherokee,* and *Seminole* in the New True Book series and *Australia* and *The Philippines* in the Enchantment of the World series. She has traveled to all seven continents and is interested in photography as well as writing.